Contents

A YEAR WITH MY CAMERA

Workbook 1

First published in 2016 by Emma Davies

ISBN: 978-0-9956324-0-0

EmmaDaviesPhotography.com

For everyone who has ever been in a car with me when we have had to stop and take a photograph.

THE ONLY PHOTOGRAPHER
I WILL COMPARE MYSELF TO
IS THE ONE I USED TO BE

Introduction

Welcome to A Year With My Camera. Today is the start of your journey to photography mastery.

This workbook was born out of my free email workshop, which repeats every year. Every Thursday I send a lesson by email which follows the structure of this workbook. Register for the free emails at AYearWithMyCamera.com and enjoy the weekly reminders to pick up your camera.

Why this course is different

Despite what they tell you, you can't learn photography in a weekend. You might want to learn in a weekend, but it can't be done. Unlike other courses, instead of pretending you can, this course embraces the fact that you can't.

To be successful, photographers must possess a unique combination of technical skills and personal vision. You can learn about one or two of the technical skills in a weekend, but to become completely fluent, to be able to use the settings on your camera unconsciously, takes much longer. You need to be able to use the controls unconsciously if you are going to express your personal vision with your camera. You simply can't be trying to remember which aperture you need at the same time as you are attempting a creative composition.

Instead of jumping from short course to weekend workshop, from online lessons to YouTube videos, you can relax, knowing you hold in your hands everything you need to know to learn photography. In order. Broken down into manageable sized chunks.

Welcome to the long haul.

If you work through the course, completing the projects along the way, this is what will happen:

In 1 month you will understand all the manual controls on your camera.

In 3 months you will not only understand, but remember all the controls, and you will be taking photos you are proud of.

And, if you finish both books, in 12 months you will be the best photographer you know.

Most people breathe a sigh of relief at this stage, realising that they don't have to learn everything all at once. It is a very liberating approach to photography. You will start by building the foundations, the technical skills, one at a time. And then with that solid base to support you, you will grow your creativity and find your personal style.

Register for the free email version of A Year With My Camera which has a weekly summary of each lesson, and a reminder to pick up your camera, at AYearWithMyCamera.com.

The A Year With My Camera Method

1. Step by step

You will cover everything you need to know, but not all at once. Trust the process. Enjoy focussing on the single concept which will be set out in each chapter, and move on only when you've understood it.

The first part (Technical) is undoubtedly the most challenging, but it is broken down into smaller concepts, and you should just do it one step at a time.

The whole course is too long to fit into a single book. This is Book 1, and if you do a chapter a week, it should take you just over 4 months. It is important to do Book 1 in the order stated. If you go on to buy Book 2 you can work through it in any order, and it will take the rest of the year to complete.

The homework at the end of each chapter is critical. You can't learn photography just by reading a book; you actually have to put the ideas into practice. You need to build your muscle memory so that you start to be able to change the controls unconsciously. That is what you're aiming for - to be able to change the settings on your camera with your eyes closed.

Try to keep the same momentum - do something every day, every week or every fortnight. The course won't be as effective if you race through the first part in a couple of weeks, take a 3 month break and then start again. This is where signing up for my emails can help tremendously - you get a reminder and summary of that week's lesson every Thursday (sign up for free at AYearWithMyCamera.com).

2. Not competitive

The only photographer you will compare yourself to is yourself - as you were at the beginning of the course.

Many people join A Year With My Camera a bit bruised from encounters in camera clubs, Facebook groups, online forums or in-person workshops. It can be devastating to have your best work criticised, dismissed and patronised. It is soul destroying to go up against aggressive, competitive photographers in any setting, especially when you are at the start of your photographic journey.

So whilst I encourage you (I would insist, if I could) to work through this course with at least one other person (see *4. Community*), this should be collaborative, not competitive. In my online groups you are only allowed to say positive things about someone else's photograph, unless they have specifically asked for a critique. And even then it has to be constructive criticism, the kind that gives the photographer something to work on. Please carry this ethos through to your in-person collaborations. Don't compete, don't compare. Do be nice, do be kind to yourself.

3. Progress, not perfection

As you work through A Year With My Camera, please treat your progress as a journey. You don't have to master every chapter completely the first time you read it. You don't have to create a masterpiece for every homework. You won't be the best photographer you know at the end of the first week. If you are taking the chapters one step at a time, at the rate of about one a week, you are doing everything you need to. If you do the homework, you are on track. (I said 'do' the homework - that's all. Not do the best homework, or the perfect homework; just have a go.)

A quick note about making mistakes: you can't avoid them, and in fact you should search them out. I had rather you take your camera out and produce 100 photos that you immediately delete, than just *think* about taking your camera out. A camera is a complicated piece of kit, and you will be taking it off Auto from day 1. It won't be plain sailing and you should expect plenty of mistakes, failures and disappointments. This is all good. This is how you learn to use your camera. When you look at a photograph you think is bad, I want you to smile and be pleased you are making progress. Because that's one less bad photograph you have left to take.

The course is deliberately designed to have 3 longer term goals (set out in the Introduction), with weekly goals (one per chapter) along the way. Please keep your eye on the long term goals, but measure your progress by what you achieve each week. At the end of each chapter there is a checklist so you can easily see how much progress you are making. Don't forget - if you can tick off even one achievement each week, you are making progress.

4. Community

I can't recommend highly enough the benefits of building a community to support you. It might just be one other person. It might be an online group, or a real-life group. They will rejoice with you when you take a photograph you are proud of, commiserate when it won't come together, understand why you are lying on the ground under a tree in the rain for the best viewpoint, but most of all, they will give you a reason to pick up your camera again when you don't fancy it.

Consistency is what will get you to the final destination on this journey. Just being able to keep taking your camera out, week by week, month by month, will get you there. And having a community that you love being a part of will make it easy.

If you want to go fast, go alone. If you want to go far, go together. *-proverb*

On the next page you'll find a list of suggested in-person and online communities to join or create, including my own official A Year With My Camera Facebook group.

COMMUNITY

ONLINE

The official A Year With My Camera Facebook group

This is the best place to ask questions, share your images and meet other people doing the course. It's the quickest way to get in touch with me.

Find a link to the current group at AYearWithMyCamera.com/join-facebook, or search Facebook for A Year With My Camera and look for the most recent group.

Instagram

Share your images with the hashtag #AYearWithMyCamera, and search the hashtag to find other people doing the course. Follow @AYearWithMyCamera (Instagram.com/AYearWithMyCamera) for reminders about projects, settings, and information about new group challenges.

Twitter

If you're not on Instagram you can use the #AYearWithMyCamera hashtag on Twitter. From time to time I host Twitter chats. The best way to find out about them is to sign up to my weekly email (go to AYearWithMyCamera.com to join).

Blipfoto

I don't host a community on Blipfoto, but I was introduced to this photo sharing site by students doing A Year With My Camera. I include it because it is a very supportive place to share your images, whether you take them for this course or otherwise. The original Blipfoto premise was that you could post just one image a day with accompanying text, to form a journal. Although I don't post every day, when I do post, I like the discipline of choosing one photo to sum up the day.

IN PERSON

I organise regular meetups in the UK, and can help you organise a local meetup.

You can also start your own smaller group to meet regularly, or work through the course together. Ideally you should all be at about the same level, and happy to work through the course in order.

About Emma

I'm a commercial and fine art botanical photographer. In my spare time I'm a travel and landscape photographer.

I was shortlisted in the 2016 International Garden Photographer of the Year Awards.

I have been published in The Telegraph, Gardens Illustrated and by the BBC.

I have taught photography at the National Trust and The Sussex Flower School, and I run workshops from my studio on the south coast of England.

I've been teaching online since 2012. I have a Masters degree in Psychology, specialising in remote learning.

Photography isn't difficult. Anyone who can read can learn to use a DSLR. But you have to do it in the right order, and you have to practise. So this course is the ultimate beginner's photography course: absolutely everything you need to know, in the right order, but most importantly, with plenty of time built in to understand and practise each new concept.

I wrote A Year With My Camera because I was meeting so many frustrated and disappointed beginner photographers who had tried to learn to use their cameras and given up. I realised they were being promised fast results by photography instructors who didn't teach the basics in an accessible way, and more importantly, didn't allow time for the concepts to sink in before moving on.

You can find me at EmmaDaviesPhotography.com, and on social media I'm @EmmaDaviesPhoto everywhere:

Instagram.com/EmmaDaviesPhoto (and also Instagram.com/AYearWithMyCamera)

Facebook.com/EmmaDaviesPhoto

Twitter.com/EmmaDaviesPhoto

Blipfoto.com/EmmaDaviesPhoto

Read this before you start

You will need a pen

This is a workbook. It's designed to be written in, so don't hold back. Tick off what you've done as you go through so you can see the progress you've made, even when it doesn't feel like you're making any. Fill in all the boxes that start, "In my own words...". They are a key part of the learning process, to help you consolidate the lessons. Stick in photos that you take, make notes in the margin, write down questions as they occur to you so you can ask them later in the Facebook group if you've joined, or Google them if you haven't.

Course structure

The whole course (Books 1 & 2) is designed to take a year. You might be faster, or slower, it doesn't matter. What does matter is that you do little and often, preferably every week, to keep making steady progress.

If you start in January, this book should take you until mid May to finish, and then Book 2 would take the rest of the year. I send out a free email every Thursday to help you remember to take your camera out that week.

Sign up at AYearWithMyCamera.com to get the emails each week.

Book 1

Part 1: Technical - learning to use all your camera's controls

Part 2: Composition - creating compelling images

Part 3: Light - the soul of every photograph

Part 4: Creative - making the photos you see in your head

Book 2

Part 1: Editing - finishing your images

Part 2: Tripod - taking photos you can only get when you have this piece of kit

Part 3: Landscape - bringing the outdoors home with you

Part 4: Travel - storytelling and memory keeping

Part 5: Macro - getting close without making mistakes

Part 6: Sharing - printing and online sharing

You will need a camera with manual controls

You will need to be able to change the aperture, shutter speed and ISO on your camera. Any DSLR or mirrorless camera should be fine, and most bridge cameras. Don't buy a new camera just to do the course: wait until you've finished part 1, when you'll understand what to look for. More information about buying a new camera can be found here: EmmaDaviesPhotography.com/new-dslr.

Video course

If you're someone who likes to learn by watching as well as reading, you might like the video version of A Year With My Camera. I have recorded all the lessons with demonstrations and plenty of examples. All the details, including a sample lesson, are at AYearWithMyCamera.com/video.

Questions?

If you have questions about the course, or about any of the lessons, the quickest place to reach me is in the official Facebook group (go to AYearWithMyCamera.com/join-facebook to find the current group).

If you need to know how to do something on your particular camera, you can either use Google, or look it up in your camera manual. I've got a list of quick downloads for most camera manuals on this page: AYearWithMyCamera.com/manuals.

Is this a photo a day course?

No. This course is not a Project 365, where you have to take a photo every day for a year. I have mixed feelings about P365s. In some respects it is a good discipline to get into, to take photographs regularly, no matter what your current mood. But I think the pressure of a daily photograph can get to be overwhelming, and take all the joy out of photography. I've done two P365s, and often found myself hating my camera and myself for not having creative ideas every day. I don't think that is the right mindset to be in, to grow as a photographer.

Practice

You can't learn to use your camera by reading a book. You must do the homework at the end of each chapter if you want to reach the goals of understanding your camera's controls by the end of the month, taking photos you are proud of by the end of 3 months, and being the best photographer you know by the end of the year.

Pre-course checklist

There are a few things you need to have done before you start. Turn over to find them on the pre-course checklist. Please don't start until you've ticked them all off.

A few essentials

Formatting memory cards

To lessen the likelihood of damage to your card and lost images, it is best to format your memory card, rather than just manually deleting your images.

1. Download all your images from your memory card, and back them up to at least one other place. I download all my images to 2 external hard drives, and I also backup key photos to the cloud.

2. Instead of using your computer to delete the images from your memory card, or deleting them one by one in your camera, use the "Format card" function on your camera. Put the card back in your camera, find the formatting option in the menus (use your manual), and format the card. It will delete all the images and prepare the card to be used again with that camera. You should also format your cards if you ever switch them between different cameras.

Turn the flash off

On-camera flash creates harsh shadows and flat photos. You are working through this book so you can create photographs with beautiful, sculpted shadows, full of depth, texture and interest. Only three of the exercises in this book are designed to be done with the flash on, so turn off your on-camera flash before you start. The flash will destroy the beautiful natural light you are using, and make many of the manual control exercises meaningless.

If your flash keeps popping up even though you think you've turned it off, it may be because you are on "Auto" mode rather than "Program" mode. Program mode gives you fully-automatic settings, but allows you to disable the flash. Auto mode on many cameras doesn't allow the flash to be disabled.

How to focus your camera

When you look through the viewfinder, you'll see a few squares or rectangles scattered across the screen. These are your focus points. When you are using auto focus, one or more of them will light up when you take a photograph to indicate that that part of the image is in focus. If you half-press the shutter button, the camera will focus without taking a photograph so you can check the correct part of the image is in focus.

Sometimes the camera gets it wrong. It usually assumes you want to focus on whatever is in the middle of the frame. If that's not the case you can either switch over to manual focus and turn the lens yourself to get the focus right, or use the focus-recompose method. This is where you frame the shot so that the camera will focus on the correct part of the scene, half press the shutter button to get the focus, then reframe the photograph by moving the camera (but holding the shutter button half pressed) until you are ready to take the image. This is an advanced technique, so don't feel you have to understand it right now. I include it here so that you can work out why your camera isn't focussing correctly when it happens.

Which lens should you use?

Start with what you have. Finish the whole of Part 1 before you buy any new kit, and if you do want to invest in another lens don't forget second hand lenses can be great value. Read Appendix 3 for more information on the characteristics of different lenses.

Pre course checklist

☐ I have downloaded my camera manual (AYearWithMyCamera.com/manuals)

☐ I have found my camera's battery charger

☐ I know how to put my memory card in (check your manual)

☐ I know how to download images from memory card to computer

☐ I know how to format my memory card (check your manual)

☐ I have turned my on-camera flash off (check your manual)

☐ I know how to focus my camera (check your manual)

☐ I am shooting Large JPEGs or RAW (read Appendix 2)

☐ I have read the section, "The A Year With My Camera Method"

☐ I know I can't learn photography in a weekend

☐ I want to learn photography step by step

☐ I will do the homework

☐ I have 3 longer term goals: to understand my camera controls, to take photos I am proud of, and to be the best photographer I know

☐ I will focus on the short term goals set out in each chapter, knowing they will get me to my long term goals if I am consistent

☐ I have signed up for the free weekly email at AYearWithMyCamera.com

PART 1: TECHNICAL

Getting the exposure correct is the first critical skill to master. Is your image too dark? Too light? Just right? This part takes you from pressing the shutter on Auto mode and getting an image with no idea what happened, to being able to control every element of the image making process.

1: Introduction to exposure

A black cat in a coal cellar is the trickiest photo you'll ever take

Aperture, shutter speed, ISO. Auto, Program, Manual. Auto exposure, exposure compensation. How often have you tried to understand all of these camera controls?

By the end of today you will have begun to understand one of them: exposure. Exposure is the foundation on which all of the camera controls are built. In the coming weeks you will pick apart each of the other terms, one at a time, so you understand everything before you move on. But for today you are going to get to grips with exposure, and nothing else.

In this chapter

When your camera takes a photo, light comes in through the lens and falls on the sensor, where the image is recorded.

The camera is able to measure the amount of light coming in to make sure the correct amount hits the sensor. This is what *exposure* means - how much light is needed on the sensor so that the photograph is not too dark or too light.

In this chapter you will learn one thing - how does the camera decide what the correct amount of light is for each photograph it takes?

This concept is often left until the end of many photography courses, because it's not straightforward. But if you understand it right at the beginning, all the remaining chapters will be much easier to follow and your progress will be much quicker.

If it doesn't all sink in first time through, that's fine. Read it at least twice, do the homework, and then move on - even if you don't fully understand everything. But keep coming back to it during the year, until you have the "Aha!" moment, and you can explain to a 7 year old how to take a picture of a black cat in a coal cellar.

(Have you read the section on page vi, "Read This Before You Start"? If not, please do it now - it will help you in the long run.)

3

What exactly is your camera doing when it takes a photo?

The very expensive computer in your camera measures how much light is falling on whatever it is you want to take a photograph of, and then makes sure it lets in exactly the right amount of light through the lens and onto the sensor so that you end up with a photo that is not too light or not too dark. This example is a white paper origami crane on a white background:

CORRECTLY EXPOSED

OVER EXPOSED

UNDER EXPOSED

How does it work?

How does the camera know which of those 3 images is the correctly exposed one? Take a minute to think about it. It doesn't have a consciousness to tell it which is an acceptable exposure, and which would be considered too dark or too light, so how does it do it?

Had a think?

The answer is in the programming. What has it been programmed to expose for? Bear in mind that it doesn't know if it is taking a photo of an origami crane, a raindrop on a leaf, or indeed a black cat in a coal cellar. How does it decide?

The answer to this is that it doesn't. And this is where it starts to make mistakes, and where you need to take control of the exposure.

Have you heard about 18% grey? Your camera is programmed to assume every image is made up of an average tone of about 18% grey.

This is a tone composed of approximately 18% grey:

This is the most critical thing you will learn on this course, so take a moment to digest it.

Every image you take, on auto modes, will default to an overall tone of that grey box. Whether you're taking a dark and moody scene or a bright and airy scene, your camera has been programmed to assume something different: a mid-grey average tone.

And that's why you're reading this. You are going to learn how to override the camera's programming, so that when you are faced with a scene that is NOT a mid grey tone, you can tell the camera what's going on. When you take control, you will stop getting over or under exposed images.

Your camera will have been programmed to assume the overall tone of every image you ever take should be this mid grey tone:

What's overall tone?

It's the average of all the tones in the image.

So if you turn your image to black and white and then either blur it, or add up all the different tones of pixel, that's the overall tone.

Here's the correctly exposed origami, gradually reduced to its overall grey tone. This is what the camera sees when it looks at the world:

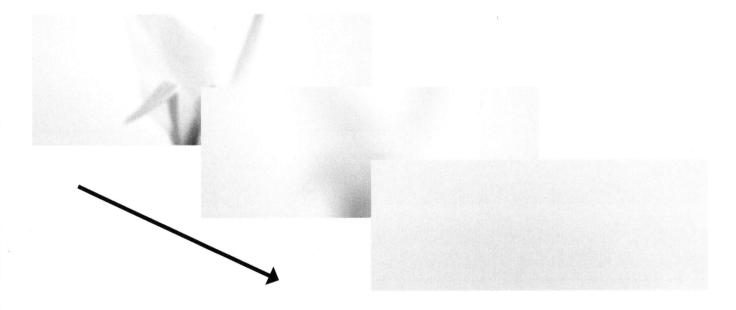

This is what the camera sees when it looks at the origami.

This is the tone that the camera is programmed to turn every photograph into, including the origami.

Without any help from the photographer, the camera will *underexpose* this photograph. It is trying to make the image have an overall tone of approximately 18% grey, even though that's not what you want:

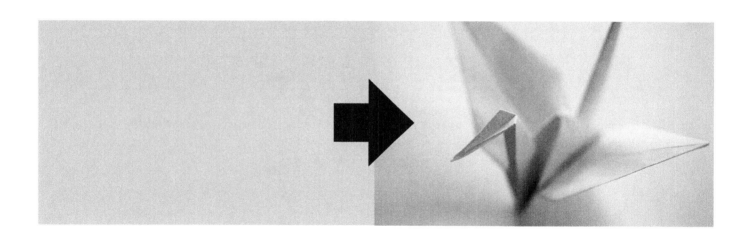

Just remember that on Auto modes, the camera will expose every image as if it is made up of that 18% grey tone. And that's not always what you want.

So we come to the black cat in the coal cellar. You should be able to work out how the camera will see this image, by now:

What tone will the camera see the black cat in the coal cellar?

Yes. 18% grey. Overexposed:

Your camera on auto or program mode turns EVERYTHING to 18% grey, whether you want it to or not.

Your job now as a photographer is to:

1. decide whether your scene is going to be approximately 18% grey in tone; and

2. if it's not, decide what you're going to do about it so that you don't end up with an over or under exposed image.

So what *can* you do about it?

You can take control away from the camera, and override its desire to turn everything it sees to a mid-grey tone.

There are 3 controls you'll learn about in the rest of this section - aperture, shutter speed and ISO. Each one allows you (or the camera) to let more (or less) light in through the lens and onto the sensor to create your image. On Program or Auto modes, the camera makes all the decisions. But you can go "off auto" and take control of these settings for yourself.

In the next chapter you'll go off auto as you learn about aperture. For now all you need to understand is that the camera is programmed to expose every scene so that it has an overall tone of about 18% grey, and that there is a solution, which you'll learn in the rest of the book.

In my own words...

Check that you've understood the most important part of this chapter. Explain here, in your own words, why a camera on an auto mode will over expose a photo of a black cat in a coal cellar.

_____

_____

_____

_____

_____

_____

_____

_____

Homework

Take 2 photos: one of a piece of white paper, and one of a piece of black paper (use the pages at the end of the book if you don't have paper at home). The aim is to show how the camera will assume each is a mid-grey tone, and create a grey exposure instead of a white/black one.

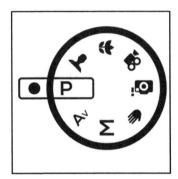

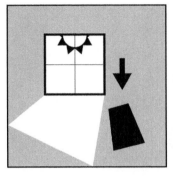

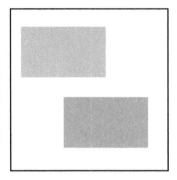

1. Leave your camera on P (Program) or A (Auto) mode.

2. Make sure each piece of paper is lit in the same way, ideally by placing it next to a window during daylight, but not in direct sunlight. No shadows on the paper, no highlights, and no reflections.

3. Fill the frame with the paper for each shot, so the whole image is either the white paper or the black paper. There shouldn't be any table or background showing.

4. When you've taken the two photographs you should notice that both images are approximately the same shade of mid grey. If they're not, read through the troubleshooting steps below.

Troubleshooting

Does your paper fill the frame?

If there is anything else in the photo - table, pens, lens cap, shadow - then the camera isn't looking at a completely uniform tone. Try again, and make sure that all you can see through the viewfinder is a rectangle of white (or black) paper.

Are you on auto or program mode?

This exercise is designed to show you that the camera defaults to a mid grey tone, no matter what you are taking a photograph of. You must be on one of the automatic modes for it to work. Double check your dial is set to "P" or "Auto".

Camera won't focus, or won't take a photo

Because you are filling the frame with a monotone, your camera might have trouble finding something to focus on. It doesn't matter whether or not the paper is in focus for this exercise, so just put your lens onto Manual Focus for now, and take the photo. Don't forget to switch it back to Auto Focus when you're done. (Look on the side of the lens for the "MF/AF" switch, or if your camera uses the menu system, use your manual to work out how to switch to manual focus.)

Stick your 2 homework photos here:

Checklist for Chapter 1

☐ I understand that the camera can measure how much light is falling on a scene

☐ I understand that the camera doesn't know what it is looking at

☐ I understand that the camera is programmed to turn every image to an approximate 18% grey tone

☐ I understand that not every scene I look at will be made up of an approximate 18% grey tone

☐ I know that a very dark scene (eg a black cat in a coal cellar) is made up of dark tones, and a camera on auto mode will therefore *overexpose* it (trying to turn it to the lighter 18% grey tone)

☐ I know that a very light scene (eg a polar bear in the snow) is made up of light tones, and a camera on auto mode will therefore *underexpose* it (trying to turn it into the darker 18% grey tone)

☐ I've done the homework: taken 2 photos, one of white paper and one of black paper

☐ I've signed up to get the Thursday emails at AYearWithMyCamera.com (this is the last reminder)

WE ARE WHAT WE REPEATEDLY DO. EXCELLENCE, THEN, IS NOT AN ACT BUT A HABIT

~ ATTRIBUTED TO ARISTOTLE

2: Aperture

Aperture - the reason you bought your big camera

As well as controlling how much light hits the sensor, the aperture affects the depth of field of your photograph. This is one of the most creative aspects of photography, and once you can control it you are well on your way to being able to call yourself a photographer.

In this chapter

In the previous chapter you learnt about the absolute basics of exposure. How the camera sees the world as grey, and how it is programmed to turn every photo it takes into an average, 18% grey tone.

You had a go at taking photos which should have been all white or all black. You saw how - if left to its own devices - the camera will turn both your white paper and your black paper to a mid grey tone.

Hold onto that knowledge - we'll be coming back to it in Chapter 5. Before we bring it all together, you need to understand 3 other things: aperture, shutter speed and ISO. These are the 3 controls that the camera uses to *change* how much light reaches the sensor when it takes a photograph.

We're going to cover them a chapter at a time, starting today with aperture.

The aperture is an adjustable hole in the lens that can get bigger or smaller, to let in more light or less light. When you change the size of the aperture you not only change how much light is coming in, you also change the *depth of field* of the photograph. And that's what you'll learn about in this chapter.

13

What is aperture?

The image-making process (on auto or program modes) goes like this:

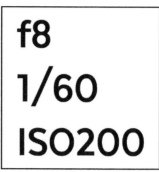

1. The camera measures how much light there is

2. The camera calculates how much light it needs to make the 18% grey image

3. The camera chooses an aperture, shutter speed and ISO which, combined, will create the 18% grey image

4. You press the shutter and get your photo

The aperture is one of the 3 things the camera has at its disposal to control the amount of light hitting the sensor and create an exposure:

- the *aperture* is a hole in the lens which can be made bigger or smaller

- the *shutter speed* is a curtain across the sensor which opens and closes to let light through

- the *ISO* is a measure of how sensitive the sensor is to light

Why does the camera need 3 different options? Why not just one?

This is the why you have a DSLR, not just a phone camera.

The 3 different options don't just control the amount of light hitting the sensor, they all have a creative effect. And aperture's creative effect is to be able to affect how much of the image is in focus, also known as the *depth of field* of an image.

With shutter speed, you can affect how sharp an image is, and the ISO affects the amount of "noise" or grain in your image.

Imagine you're taking a photograph of a beach. You're standing on the beach, pointing your camera straight towards the sunset, with a person walking away from you in the distance. Now imagine a line running directly away from you, towards the horizon. It starts at your feet, travels across the sand, and carries on all the way to the sunset, passing over the person:

This imaginary line is called the depth of field. And the size of the aperture affects which section of that line will be sharply focussed* in your image. You can decide whether to have everything in focus in the picture, from the sand to the sun. Or whether you just want the person to be in focus.

To have a *large* depth of field, you choose a *small* aperture.

To have a *small* depth of field, you choose a *large* aperture.

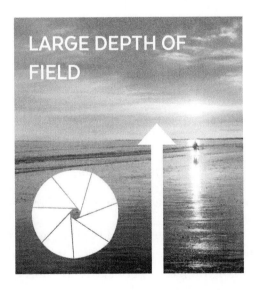

Technically, the depth of field is which part of the line is "acceptably sharp" to the naked eye - not necessarily what's actually in focus. The two are slightly different. However, you'll often see depth of field defined as what's "in focus".

Aperture priority mode

For this chapter, ignore the fact that aperture affects exposure. Today you are just concentrating on the extra creative effect that aperture has - the ability to affect depth of field. The most common use of depth of field is to blur the background. This is achieved by making sure only the subject falls within the sharp depth of field range, and the background is outside it.

(And this is where 90% of DSLR owners give up. You are not going to be one of the 90%. Read on, understand, and enjoy.)

The next thing you are going to ignore, for today, is that your camera (actually, your lens) probably has around 20 different aperture settings. *You are only going to look at the biggest and the smallest.*

Before you try the homework you'll need to find out what the biggest and smallest apertures are on the lens you are using. If it's the first time you've done this, find your camera manual:

1. Download (or find) your manual.

If you can't find it, I have links to all the major manufacturer's manuals on my website, at AYearWithMyCamera.com/manuals.

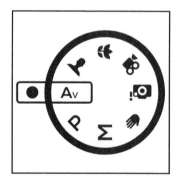

2. Find out how to put your camera onto aperture priority mode.

(Or just Google it. eg. "How do I put a Canon 6D onto aperture priority mode?") Hint: for most cameras you just turn the dial that has P, M, S and A on it, to A. Or Av. 'A' usually stands for Aperture, not Auto.

Do it. Put your camera on aperture priority mode. You are now off auto, congratulations.

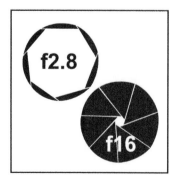

3. Go back to the manual and find out how change the aperture.

Now, scroll through all the aperture settings from beginning to end. Write down the 2 numbers that will be at each end of the list. They might be 5.6 and 11. They might be 2.8 and 16. If you have a very expensive lens they might be 1.2 and 32. (If you are using a zoom lens, pick one end of the zoom and do the whole exercise either zoomed all the way in, or all the way out. The min and max apertures will probably change as you zoom, and I don't want this to confuse you.)

The min and max apertures for my lenses

Write down the name of your lens (eg. 50mm or 35-70mm), and the smallest and biggest apertures for each. You can find the name of your lens by looking around the front of it for a number with "mm" after it.

eg 50mm: min aperture = f32, max aperture = f1.6

_____

_____

_____

_____

What are the f numbers?

The aperture settings are called f-numbers, or f-stops.

These are all the f-stops, in complete increments, in order, from the largest size (smallest number) to the smallest size (largest number). You just have to remember that the large hole = the smallest number, and the small hole = the largest number. No easy way round that.

f1.4 > f2 > f2.8 > f4 > f5.6 > f8 > f11 > f16 > f22 > f32

Your camera might give you apertures of f7.1, or f10. These are just fractional f-stops, between the full increments. (Like 2.5 comes between 2 and 3.)

Appendix 1 has a list of all the apertures, full and fractional. I suggest you take a photo of Appendix 1 so you always have it on your phone.

Homework

Take 2 photos which are exactly the same, except for the aperture. The aim is to see what depth of field is, and how your aperture can control it. This works best with a single subject, like a flower or a cup, set up with a plain background some distance away. You should be able to blur the background with your large aperture photo.

You also need to know that the depth of field starts from the point you focus on, and extends in front and behind that point - so it's very important that you focus on your subject for this exercise, not on the background.

There's no rush. Take it step by step. Go onto aperture priority, dial in f4 or whatever your smallest number is, find your well-lit subject, focus on it, take the photo. Do the same with f16 or whatever your largest number is.

| 1. You'll need a brightly lit place, ideally out of doors, so you can work with your smallest aperture easily. | 2. Take your first photo on aperture priority, focussing on your subject, and with the largest aperture (smallest number). | 3. Take exactly the same photo, but with the smallest aperture (largest number). | 4. Your first photo should have a small depth of field and your second photo should have a large depth of field. |

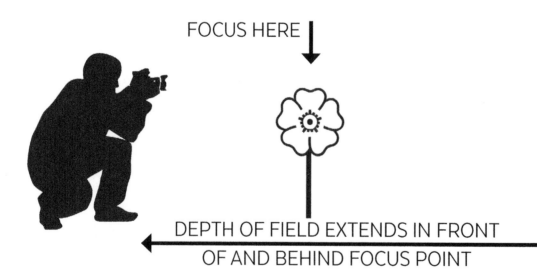

FOCUS HERE

DEPTH OF FIELD EXTENDS IN FRONT
OF AND BEHIND FOCUS POINT

Troubleshooting

How close are you to the subject?

With a normal lens (50mm or so), don't stand too far away from the subject. Around a metre, maybe a bit more. If it's really not working, get as close as you can to the subject and still be able to focus on the subject.

How close is the subject to the background?

It needs to be probably at least a metre away, but if it won't blur, try moving the subject further away from the background.

What exactly is your largest number aperture?

If your largest number aperture is f5.6 or f8, you probably aren't going to see the blurred background effect unless you look very closely at your photo, or move the subject a very long way from the background and stand as close as possible to the subject to take the photo. If you have a cheaper kit lens (one that came bundled with the camera), you might get frustrated with not having a wide maximum aperture to be able to take these kinds of photos. If that's the case, you may have outgrown your first piece of kit. Have a look at a 50mm f1.8 or f2.8, if you want a reasonably priced lens with a wide maximum aperture. But finish Part 1 before you buy any new kit.

What lens are you using?

The effect appears more pronounced with longer lenses (100mm and longer). Wide angle lenses (35mm and wider) do create the effect, but you have to stand very, very close to the subject for it to work.

Have you focussed on the subject?

Are you quite sure? There's no chance you could accidentally have focussed on the background, or foreground? Put the subject right in the middle of the photo, fill the frame as much as you can, and try again. Switch to manual focus if you need to, and focus by turning the ring on the lens (check your manual for details).

Photograph is completely over exposed

If you are working with your largest size aperture (smallest number, eg f4), there might simply be too much light for your camera to cope with. You've effectively reached the mechanical limits of your camera. Solution: move somewhere darker - even just into the shade will help.

Photograph is completely under exposed

The opposite happens with your smallest aperture (eg f22). Move somewhere brighter.

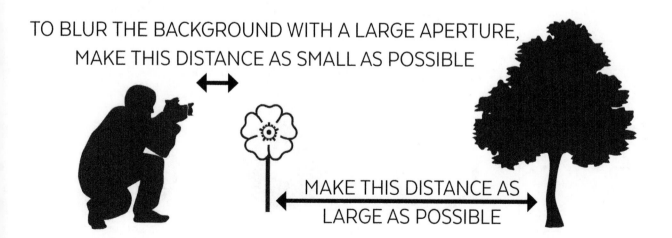

TO BLUR THE BACKGROUND WITH A LARGE APERTURE, MAKE THIS DISTANCE AS SMALL AS POSSIBLE

MAKE THIS DISTANCE AS LARGE AS POSSIBLE

1.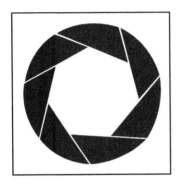

This aperture is most likely to be:

A f4

B f16

C f32

2.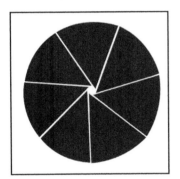

This aperture is most likely to be:

A f4

B f5.6

C f16

3.

f8?

Which of these size apertures best represents f8?

A  B   C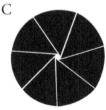

4.

f2.8?

Which of these size apertures best represents f2.8?

A   B   C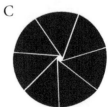

5. If the photographer is focussing on the flower, with an aperture of f2.8, what is the tree in the background likely to be?

A Blurred   B Not blurred

6. If the photographer is focussing on the flower, with an aperture of f32, what is the tree in the background likely to be?

A Blurred   B Not blurred

7. Which of these apertures gives the largest depth of field?

A f2.8   B f8   C f22

8. Which of these apertures gives the smallest depth of field?

A f4   B f5.6   C f11

Stick your 2 homework photos here:

Checklist for Chapter 2

☐ I can put my camera on Aperture Priority mode

☐ I can change my apertures

☐ I know what the smallest and largest apertures are for each of my lenses

☐ I know that aperture is one of the 3 ways that my camera controls the amount of light coming in through the lens and hitting the sensor

☐ I know that the aperture is found in the lens, not in the camera

☐ I know that f4 is a large aperture and that f16 is a small aperture

☐ I know that the depth of field is the section of an image which is acceptably sharp

☐ I know that f4 will give a small depth of field and that f16 will give a large depth of field

☐ I can take a photo of a subject with the background blurred:

DONE IS BETTER THAN PERFECT

3: Shutter speed

Shutter speed - playing with time

If you need sharp photos, or you want some motion blur, you'll want to understand how shutter speed affects what records on your sensor.

In this chapter

We have covered 18% grey - how the camera sees the world. It turns every photo it takes to an average grey tone. Usually that's OK, but sometimes (if you're taking very light or very dark photos), it gives dreadfully exposed images.

In the previous chapter you learned about aperture - the small hole in the lens. If you make it a big hole, not only will it let in more light, but it will also reduce the depth of field (the amount of the photograph in sharp focus). If you make it a small hole, it will let in less light and also increase the depth of field.

In this chapter you'll look at *shutter speed*.

Shutter speed is one of the other things the camera (or you) has under its control. And, just like aperture, as well as being able to control the amount of light hitting the sensor, it has its own creative effect.

With shutter speed, you get control over the amount of blur, or sharpness, in the image. Sometimes you want blur, sometimes you don't. The camera doesn't know whether you do or don't, and it will always, always pick a mid range shutter speed by default. So if you want anything at the extremes - a very blurred image, or a super sharp image, you have to take control.

Fast or slow shutter speed?

The shutter is a curtain that opens and closes in front of the sensor.

A fast shutter speed opens and closes fast. A slow shutter speed opens and closes more slowly.

Can you see that if your subject moves whilst the shutter is open (a slow shutter speed), it will record as a blur? (And also - if *you* move while the shutter is open, you'll cause a blur in the photo even if the subject isn't moving. This is called camera shake.)

And can you see that if your shutter opens and closes in a fraction of a second - faster than the subject is moving - you will be able to freeze the action?

SLOW SHUTTER SPEED   FAST SHUTTER SPEED

What are the shutter speeds?

These are common shutter speeds, in complete increments, in order from the slowest (lets most light in) to the fastest (lets least light in). They are measured in fractions of a second.

1/15 > 1/30 > 1/60 > 1/125 > 1/250 > 1/500 > 1/1000

Your camera might give you different shutter speeds, like 1/50th or 1/160th. These are just fractional speeds, between full increments. (Like 2.5 comes between 2 and 3).

Appendix 1 has a list of all the shutter speeds, full and fractional.

Shutter priority mode

Before you do the homework, you'll need to know how to change your shutter speed.

1. *Download (or find) your manual.*

I have links to all the major manufacturer's manuals on my website, at AYearWithMyCamera.com/manuals.

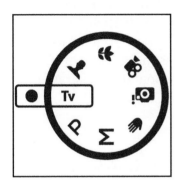

2. *Find out how to put your camera onto shutter priority mode.*

This is where you choose the shutter speed, and the camera will pick an aperture. (Google it if you don't want to read your manual: "How to put a Fuji XT1 onto shutter priority mode".)

Do it. Put your camera on shutter priority mode.

3. *Go back to the manual and find out how change the shutter speed.*

Shutter speeds are measured in fractions of a second, and will be displayed either as "60" or "1/60" (for 1/60th of a second).

Homework

Take 2 photos of the same moving subject, one with a fast and one with a slow shutter speed. The aim is to see what effect changing your shutter speed has on the blur that is recorded in the final image.

 1/2 1/500

1. You'll need a brightly lit place, ideally out of doors, so you can work with your fastest shutter speed easily.

2. Take your first photo on shutter priority, focussing on your subject, and with a slow shutter speed (try something very slow like 1 second, or 1/2 sec).

3. Take exactly the same photo, but with a very fast shutter speed. Try the fastest possible with the available light you have, at least 1/500th, but 1/1000th if you can manage it.

4. You should get one blurred image, and one very sharp image (or at least, your subject is sharp - don't worry about the background).

Pick a subject that's moving reasonably fast - someone running (across the frame, not towards you), a car (careful where you stand), something blowing in the wind, water running from a tap, your dog, or even just someone's waving hand up close.

Slow shutter speed

1.3 seconds

28

Troubleshooting

You should get one photo where the subject is blurred (the one with the longer shutter speed), and one where the subject is sharp (the one with the shorter shutter speed). If not, try these tips:

Camera won't take a photo at a fast shutter speed

You don't have enough light - the faster shutter speeds let in only a tiny amount of light and your camera might just refuse to take a photo if there isn't enough light. Try at 1/500th and see if you can get the effect you want, otherwise go outside during the day in a well-lit place.

Focus won't work

It can be hard to keep your focus on the subject when the subject is fast-moving. Don't worry too much about the focus for this exercise. As long as you can take two photographs, one with a blur and one without, it doesn't matter if your focus is off. Try switching to manual focus if you want to get it right

Photograph is completely over exposed

If you are working with a long shutter speed (like a whole second or more), there might simply be too much light for your camera to cope with. Just like when you worked with large apertures, you've effectively reached the mechanical limits of your camera. Solution: move somewhere darker.

Photograph is completely under exposed

The opposite happens with your faster shutter speeds (eg 1/1000th or faster). Move somewhere brighter.

Fast shutter speed

1/320th second

Stick your 2 homework photos here:

Checklist for Chapter 3

☐ I can put my camera on Shutter Priority mode

☐ I can change my shutter speeds

☐ I know that shutter speed is one of the 3 ways that my camera controls the amount of light coming in through the lens and hitting the sensor

☐ I know that the shutter is found in the camera, just in front of the sensor

☐ I know that a whole second is a very long shutter speed

☐ I know that 1/2000th second is a very short shutter speed

☐ I know that shutter speed affects the amount of blur, or camera shake, in an image

☐ I know that a shutter speed of a whole second will create lots of blur if either the subject or the camera is moving

☐ I can take a photo with the subject blurred:

GREAT THINGS ARE DONE BY A SERIES OF SMALL THINGS BROUGHT TOGETHER

~ VINCENT VAN GOGH

4: ISO

The easiest part of exposure to understand

Once you know what it is, you can forget about ISO for most of the time. But when you need it, you'll be glad you know how to use it.

In this chapter

The camera has 3 options when it comes to controlling the amount of light hitting the sensor and making the photograph: aperture, shutter speed and ISO.

The first two are mechanical options that physically control the amount of light. ISO is digital.

The ISO is the degree of sensitivity of the sensor. It can be changed between photos, and is best seen as a useful backup option to have in extreme light conditions (very bright or very dark).

The most difficult thing to learn when it comes to ISO is how to change it. On many cameras you have to hold a button and turn a dial at the same time. It's a critical skill to learn though, and it will come easily with practice.

What is ISO?

ISO (stands for International Standards Organisation) is a *measure of sensitivity*.

In the days of film cameras, the film you chose had a fixed sensitivity to light, called the ISO. A low ISO (50) was used in very bright conditions (not very sensitive to light). A high ISO (1600) was used in darker conditions (more sensitive to light).

Nowadays, ISO refers to the sensitivity of the sensor to light. In the days of film you were stuck with the same ISO until you'd finished your roll of 24 or 36 shots. If you moved from the beach to inside a museum, your ISO would be wrong. But with digital, you can change the ISO for every shot if you want to.

Why not just stick your ISO on high and leave it?

The downside of using a high ISO (very sensitive) is the noise. In the days of film, it was called grain, and made those arty black and white shots so memorable.

Nowadays it's not as attractive, and the amount of noise that you get is entirely dependent on how expensive your camera was. You might have wondered why some cameras are so much more expensive - one reason is the quality of the

sensor, and the degree to which the image quality deteriorates with noise at higher ISOs.

So, whilst aperture and shutter speed had creative effects as well as affecting the amount of light reaching the sensor, ISO really just has a potential downside. Remember that the higher ISO you use, the more the quality of your photo will degrade.

A high ISO lets more light in (like having a wide aperture or a slow shutter speed), but the quality of your photograph will deteriorate due to noise.

How to change ISO

There is no 'ISO priority mode', like you have aperture or shutter priority modes.

Exactly how to change your ISO will depend on your camera, so make sure you have your manual ready. Some cameras have a button or a dial to change the ISO: for others it's accessed through a menu.

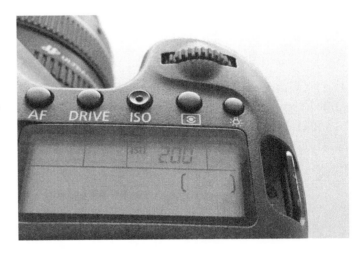

The easiest method - Auto ISO

If your camera is newer (or more expensive), you might have Auto ISO mode. This means that whatever mode you are using, the camera will automatically choose the lowest possible ISO.

You can also change the defaults in the settings, to limit the upper ISO. This is useful if you definitely don't want to go above a certain ISO. I usually have my upper ISO set to 400 for a professional shoot, and no limit for personal shoots. On professional shoots the quality of the images is critical, and I must use other ways of getting the shot rather than relying on high ISOs, but for personal work I'd often rather get the shot no matter what the ISO.

Just be aware that on some cameras, on some modes, Auto ISO won't work. For example, it might only work on Program or Auto mode, not on Shutter or Aperture priority. This is where you need to read your manual. First, find out if you have Auto ISO. Then find out if there are any times when it won't work.

Manual ISO

If you don't have Auto ISO, you'll need to know how to change your ISO manually. Look it up. It's probably a button on the top of your camera (marked "ISO"), and then one of the dials to increase/decrease. Don't forget to put it back to a lowish ISO (200) once you've finished.

When to change ISO

You might have noticed, especially on the shutter speed exercise in the last chapter, that when you were at extremes (very high or low shutter speed), you got images that were too bright or too dark (over exposed or under exposed).

This happened because your camera had reached its mechanical limits. If you were outside and using a very long shutter speed during the middle of the day, your camera would have selected the tiniest aperture possible to compensate for the very long shutter speed. But at some point, it would not be able to make the aperture any smaller, and because you were using a long shutter speed, light would continue to pour into the camera and onto the sensor, overexposing the photograph.

In this situation, you need to make the ISO LESS sensitive to light (make it a smaller number). It's like putting a pair of sunglasses on your camera's sensor - a low ISO lets it cope with very bright conditions.

Alternatively, if you were on aperture priority and using a tiny aperture to get a big depth of field, at some point your camera will not be able to use a long enough shutter speed to compensate, and your image will be too dark. Or, more likely, you won't want to use a longer shutter speed because you'll get camera shake.

In this case, if you didn't have a tripod to allow you to use a long shutter speed, you'd increase your ISO to make the sensor *more* sensitive to light.

Homework

Step 1

Work out how to change your ISO manually. Also find out if you have Auto ISO, and whether it doesn't work on any of your modes.

Step 2

Pick either the shutter speed or aperture exercise from the last 2 chapters, and do it again but with ISO as a backup. View your photos on a computer screen at 100% so you can check the noise.

Let's say you decide to try the shutter speed exercise again. On your fastest shutter speed (let's say 1/2000th), you might have found your images too dark. Go into your ISO settings, and change your ISO to it's highest possible setting (eg ISO 12,800). Don't worry about the fact your images will be full of noise - the purpose of this exercise is just to see how changing your ISO gives you a backup option.

For the slow shutter speed (eg. 1 second), change your ISO to the lowest possible setting (eg ISO 100). The effect won't be as noticeable at the low settings because your camera will already be picking a low ISO for you if possible. With some cameras you might find the lowest ISO is something like 200, but that you can take it down to 100 or even 50 by changing a custom function or one of the menu settings. Check your manual, because this is a very useful option when you're working in very bright conditions.

For the aperture settings: for the biggest aperture (smallest number, eg. f4), you'll need to reduce the sensitivity of the sensor to compensate for all that light pouring in, so pick a low ISO (ISO 100). For the smallest aperture (biggest number, eg. f22), you'll want to increase the sensitivity of the sensor, so pick a high ISO (ISO 12,800).

What are the ISO settings?

These are the ISO settings, in complete increments, in order from the least sensitive (lets least light in; use in bright conditions) to the most sensitive (lets most light in; use in dark conditions).

50 > 100 > 200 > 400 > 800 > 1600 > 3200 > 6400 > 12800

Your camera might give you ISOs of eg. 160, or 500. These are just fractional ISO measurements, between the full increments. (Like 2.5 comes between 2 and 3.)

Appendix 1 has a list of all the ISO settings, full and fractional.

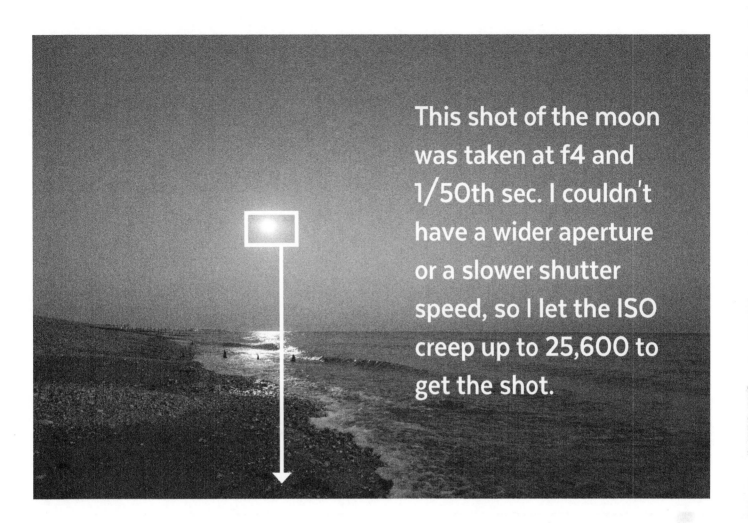

This shot of the moon was taken at f4 and 1/50th sec. I couldn't have a wider aperture or a slower shutter speed, so I let the ISO creep up to 25,600 to get the shot.

When viewed at 100%, the ISO 25,600 image is full of noise.

Stick your homework photos here:

Checklist for Chapter 4

☐ I know that ISO is one of the 3 ways that my camera controls the amount of light needed for a correct exposure

☐ I know that the ISO is a measure of the sensitivity of the sensor for a particular photograph

☐ I know that ISO 50 is a low sensitivity, and should be used in very bright conditions if I can't use a smaller aperture or a faster shutter speed

☐ I know that anything above ISO 1600 is a high sensitivity, and should be used in dark conditions if I can't use a wider aperture or a slower shutter speed

☐ I know that a higher ISO creates more noise in my image

☐ I can change my ISO without looking it up in the manual

☐ I have tried either the aperture or the shutter speed homework again, using ISO as a backup to help with the extreme settings

THE GREATER DANGER FOR MOST OF US LIES NOT IN SETTING OUR AIM TOO HIGH AND FALLING SHORT; BUT IN SETTING OUR AIM TOO LOW, AND ACHIEVING OUR MARK

~ ATTRIBUTED TO MICHELANGELO

5: Exposure triangle

3-way balance

Taking control, becoming a photographer.

In this chapter

You've learnt so far that exposure = aperture + shutter speed + ISO.

On auto modes (including aperture and shutter priority), your camera decides what the correct exposure is. You will remember from the first chapter that it assumes the world is made up of a single mid grey tone.

On fully auto mode, your camera decides which combination of aperture and shutter speed (and ISO, if you have Auto ISO) will be used to get the exposure it needs. And, given a chance, it will never, ever choose any settings at the extremes. You will never get the camera choosing a shutter speed of half a second; it is protecting you from camera shake. It will never pick an aperture of f2.8 or a high ISO unless it has no other option; it is protecting you from an out of focus subject and a grainy photo.

It will always pick middle of the road settings unless it is very dark or very light. You'll be stuck with f8, 1/250th and ISO200. So if you ever want to use f2.8 or f22, with a shutter speed of 1/4000th or 2 seconds, or any other combination of extreme or specific settings, you'll need to go off auto altogether.

In this chapter you'll shoot on fully Manual, take control, and you will be able to call yourself a photographer.

This is one of the most complicated chapters in the book, so please take it one step at a time. You don't need to remember everything - as long as you understand it as you are reading it, that is fine at this stage. The main concept to understand is that you can balance changes in aperture with changes in shutter speed or ISO.

What is the exposure triangle?

Imagine a 3-way seesaw (teeter-totter). If one corner goes up, the other 2 corners have to go down by an equal and opposite amount. This is exactly the same for camera settings, and it's known as the exposure triangle.

If aperture, shutter speed and ISO are the 3 corners, and one goes up (let's say you want a shallow depth of field so you pick a large aperture), then, to keep the same exposure, the other 2 need to go down to compensate. If you are on aperture priority mode, or shutter priority mode, the camera does the compensation for you. If you want complete control, you will need to shoot on Manual mode.

You don't need to shoot on Manual all the time, but to call yourself a photographer you need to know how to do it. And there will be a few occasions when you need to shoot Manual.

When should I shoot Manual?

Shoot on Manual mode when you need to control both aperture and shutter speed.

You might want both a particular depth of field (eg. you want to use f16) but you also want a little bit of motion blur, so you want a shutter speed of 1/30th. You can't afford to let the camera pick either, so you must pick both.

Or if you shooting macro (close up), you will want to have a much higher shutter speed than normally needed, because camera shake is magnified along with everything else. The camera won't know this, and will pick a mid range shutter of 1/125 or 1/250, when you actually need 1/1000th or faster.

If you need to replicate exactly the same settings between shots (for example in studio work), you would use Manual mode to fix the settings in place. In a studio you would change the amount of light being used as required, rather than changing the camera settings.

How to shoot on Manual mode

Find the "M" setting on your dial. Now dial in all 3 settings - aperture, shutter speed and ISO (unless you are using auto ISO). Use your camera manual if you need a reminder of how to change each setting.

Don't forget to put your camera back onto your preferred setting once you've finished (Program, Auto, Shutter priority or Aperture priority). If you don't do this, and aren't used to shooting on Manual, you'll take some unexpectedly over or under exposed images the next time you go out with your camera.

Understanding stops

What are stops?

Do you remember the list of aperture f-stops? And shutter speeds and ISOs? f4, f5.6, f8; 1/60th, 1/125th, 1/250th; 100, 200, 400?

The gap between these measures of aperture, shutter speed and ISO is important, and it's called a "stop".

From f4 to f5.6 is 1 stop. From 1/60th to 1/125th is 1 stop. From ISO 400 to ISO 800 is 1 stop. Each stop lets in the same amount of light. So 1 stop on the aperture scale corresponds to 1 stop on the shutter speed scale. Knowing this allows you to compensate accurately.

If the camera picked f5.6 but you want f11, that's 2 full stops smaller. f5.6 > f 8 > f11. So, to keep the same exposure, you would need to change the shutter speed by 2 full stops larger, eg. 1/500th < 1/250th < 1/125th. Or the ISO by 2 full stops larger; ISO 100 < ISO 200 < ISO 400. Or you could change the shutter speed by 1 full stop and the ISO by 1 full stop.

Full stops, half stops and third stops

The benchmark stops are the ones mentioned so far in the book. f4, f5.6, f8, f11, f16. 1/60th, 1/125th, 1/250th, 1/500th. ISO 100, 200, 400, 800. But you may find that your camera picks an aperture like f7.1, or a shutter speed of 1/160th. That's because there are stops that fall exactly half way between the benchmark full stops, and there are also stops that fall exactly a third and two thirds of the way between the benchmark full stops. Your camera will be set to show either full plus half, or full plus third stops. You can change between them.

It's not critical that you remember all the half stops and third stops, but you should be familiar with the benchmark full stops for each of the 3 settings.

In Appendix 1 you'll find all the stops - full, half and thirds. Have a quick look now.

Double the light / half the light

As you move between stops, remember that each stop lets in *twice as much light* as the one before it (rather than just +1 stop). This diagram shows the concept for apertures, so you can see the huge difference between each end of the scale:

Homework - shoot on Manual

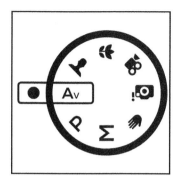

f8	f8 > f5.6	1/250 >
1/250		1/500
ISO200		

1. Select aperture priority mode, choose an aperture that's a full stop (eg f8) and take a photo.

2. Write down what settings the camera picks. Your settings might be different to these.

3. Go onto Manual mode and change the aperture by 1 stop (bigger) to have a shallower depth of field.

4. Change the shutter speed by a corresponding 1 stop in the opposite direction (faster) and take another photo.

Both the photos should have the same exposure, if the light hasn't changed and you focussed on the same spot. The only difference should be a slightly shallower depth of field in the second photo.

Have another go, this time on shutter priority. Try changing the settings by 2 stops, and by using a combination of both aperture and ISO to compensate.

This chart shows the 3 settings laid out in the same direction, from less light to more light (or for ISO, less sensitive to more sensitive), to help you with this exercise. It's important that you start on a full stop setting. Check Appendix 1 if your settings aren't shown here - you may be on a third or a half stop setting.

aperture	f16	f11	f8	f5.6	f4
shutter speed	1/1000	1/500	1/250	1/125	1/60
ISO	50	100	200	400	800

less light   more light

TEST YOURSELF

This is a difficult test. Don't expect to get full marks on your first try, or for it to take only a minute or two. Have a go, move on, but come back to it from time to time. By the end of the year you should find it straightforward.

1. Which of these is is the only full stop aperture?

A f7.1   B f5.6   C f3.5

2. Which of these are full stop shutter speeds?

A 1/60   B 1/125   C 1/400

3. To go one full stop faster (less light) from a shutter speed of 1/125, what do you need?

A 1/60   B 1/250   C 1/500

4. To go one full stop wider (more light) from an aperture of f5.6, what do you need?

A f8   B f16   C f4

5. To go 2 stops less light than f11, 1/250 and ISO 400, which combination can you use?

A f16, 1/125, ISO 400   B f11, 1/500, ISO 400   C f16, 1/250, ISO 200

6. To go 2 stops more light than f16, 1/500 and ISO 200, which combination can you use?

A f8, 1/125, ISO 100   B f8, 1/500, ISO 200   C f11, 1/1000, ISO 200

7. To go 3 stops less light than f8, 1/250 and ISO 200, which combination can you use?

A f5.6, 1/125, ISO 400   B f16, 1/60, ISO 100   C f8, 1/1000, ISO 100

8. To go 3 stops more light than f11, 1/500 and ISO 100, which combination can you use?

A f4, 1/60, ISO 800   B f16, 1/1000, ISO 50   C f8, 1/250, ISO 200

Stick one of your homework photos here:

In my own words...

Can you write down the full stops for aperture, shutter speed and ISO, in order from least light to most light?

_____

_____

_____

_____

_____

_____

Checklist for Chapter 5

☐ I know that this is one of the most difficult chapters, and that I don't need to learn it all off by heart today

☐ I understand that aperture, shutter speed and ISO are like 3 corners of a balanced triangle, and that if I change one, the other two need to change by an equal and opposite amount if I want to keep the same exposure

☐ I know that a stop of light is the amount between full increments of aperture, shutter speed and ISO

☐ I know that stops can be measured in full increments (like f5.6 and 1/60th), but also in half stops and third stops (see Appendix 1)

☐ I know that the easiest way to remember how the stops work together is to actually try to change them

☐ I have done the homework

☐ I have tried the quiz, but not felt a failure if it was really hard - I trust the fact that if I keep working through the course it will get easier

---

You don't need to understand everything about stops and shooting on Manual mode right now. If you can tick off everything in this checklist, you can move on.

TO AVOID CRITICISM, DO NOTHING, SAY NOTHING, AND BE NOTHING

~ ELBERT HUBBARD

6: Metering

The final piece of the puzzle

The question you will answer today, is this: "I know the camera gets the exposure wrong a lot (because it exposes for a mid grey tone). But how do I know what the right exposure is?"

In this chapter

So far in Part 1 you have learnt that the camera wants to turn everything mid grey, which is a problem if your subject is on the white side or on the black side overall.

You have learnt how to manipulate each of the 3 settings (aperture, shutter speed and ISO).

And in the last chapter you learnt how to start with the settings the camera picked but then switch to Manual mode and change one or all of them separately, without changing the overall exposure.

In this chapter you will learn the final piece of information you need to be able to call yourself a photographer: how to tell what the right exposure

is in the first place. It's no good being able to change the settings on Manual mode if you are just preserving an incorrect exposure. You need to be able to first decide if the camera has got it right, and then decide what settings you want.

It's a lot to remember, but you don't have to be able to do it all by the end of the chapter. And you won't always be needing to shoot on Manual or correct the camera's exposure. For now, you only have to understand it, and have had a go. Throughout the rest of the course there will be plenty of reminders and exercises to keep you practising.

What is metering?

When the camera measures how much light is falling on the scene, this is called metering. In the old days we used to use a light meter. We carefully picked a mid-grey part of the landscape, or took a reading off whatever we wanted to be correctly exposed (usually someone's face), and then translated the meter's suggested settings to suit our creative priorities.

This is still the most accurate way to get the right exposure.

But 21st century cameras pretty much do away with the need to use light meters, unless you're working in a studio. Now you can rely on the camera's built-in light meter, plus the instant histogram feedback you get.

How does the camera meter?

Just as it's critical that you know what the camera is programmed to do when it comes to fixing exposure (it turns everything mid-grey), so you also need to know what it has been programmed to do when it measures the light in first place (metering). There are 3 kinds of metering that the camera can use, and you can switch between them (check your manual). In each one, the camera is programmed to do something different.

1. *Matrix, or evaluative metering*

This is usually the default setting. The camera takes a broad reading from everywhere in the frame. Useful for beginners, but if the background is light (like the sky), and your subject is just in the middle, the light background will skew the exposure and your subject will not be correctly exposed.

2. *Centre-weighted metering*

The camera gives priority to whatever is in the middle of the frame. This is a better all-purpose setting to use, if you generally want what is in the middle of the frame to be correctly exposed.

3: *Spot metering*

You pick one very small area of the frame to take a reading from, usually one of the small rectangles that you can see in the viewfinder that the camera uses to show where it has focussed. This is the most accurate way of getting a correct exposure for a single part of the image.

Using the histogram

The histogram is a graph that shows the results of the camera's metering, in bar chart form. You can switch it on in your settings, so it will either show up in the viewfinder as you take your photo, or on the LCD as you review your photos afterwards.

This is where the magic happens. The one thing that is constant throughout all of this is the histogram. It never lies. The rest of what the camera is doing can be misleading: the exposure it makes is based off a mid-grey baseline which might not be accurate for your image. The metering will depend on which mode you have selected. You can't even rely on the LCD on your camera to be accurate because the brightness settings can be changed, and the appearance alters depending how bright or dark your surroundings are.

Don't forget your eye/brain combination also can mislead you. Your brain interprets what the eye sees and you can often think something is bright enough because it *should* be bright enough, and your eyes have got used to the dark.

You can use the histogram to check that what the camera is telling you is in fact what is in front of you. If you're taking a photo of a polar bear in the snow that is coming out grey, you can check the histogram to see what's going on. If you're taking a photo of a black dog in a black shed, you can check the histogram. And if you're just taking a photo of a sunset, a landscape, your grand-daughter or a flower, and it doesn't look quite right, you can check the histogram to see what you need to do to fix it.

Here's how. First, check your manual and change the settings so that the histogram shows as a preview in your viewfinder or on your LCD when you take a photo (look up "LCD preview", or "viewfinder preferences"). Next, start to take a photo - half press the shutter to get the focus - and see what the histogram is doing.

Lastly, look at the scene and ask yourself whether the histogram reflects what you are seeing in front of your eyes. If not, you know the camera's auto settings or metering mode have defaulted to something you don't want. You can then correct the camera's error.

What exactly is the histogram?

On the next couple of pages I'll show you how to do all this - how to interpret the histogram, check it reflects reality, and then fix anything that needs fixing. First, here's a quick explanation of what the histogram does.

The histogram is simply a bar chart showing light values. Imagine a bar chart showing how many apples, pears and oranges a shop sells in a week. If it sells 10 apples, 20 pears and 30 oranges, the bar chart will look like this:

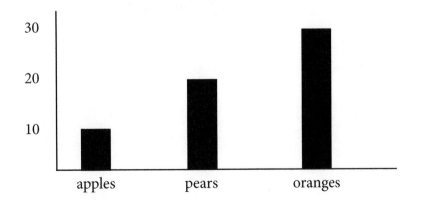

Now imagine you are looking piece of paper which has 1 black stripe, 2 grey stripes, and 3 white stripes. The bar chart would look like this:

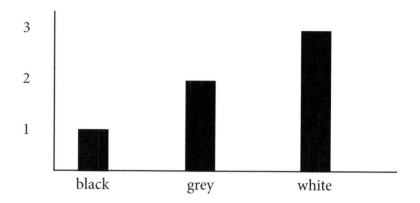

And that is all the histogram does. The camera assigns a tone value (from black to white via all the greys) to every single pixel in your image. It then plots them on a bar chart to give you your histogram. It counts all the pure black pixels and gives them a bar all the way to the left, and does the same for every shade of grey all the way to pure white over on the right.

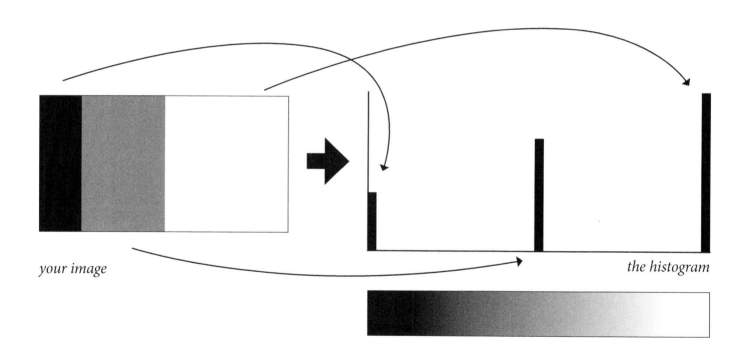

your image

the histogram

When it comes to an actual photograph, the camera just counts all the pixels, sees how many of each tone there are, and then plots them all on a bar chart:

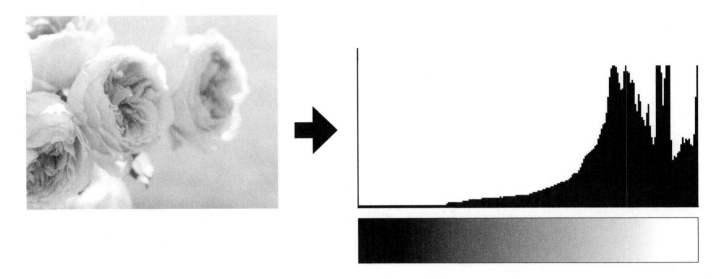

In this image the histogram is showing that there are no black and darker tones at all. Does that look right? In the original image you can still see plenty of detail in the shadows which means they are not completely black, so yes, you would not expect to see the histogram touching the left hand side of the chart.

And at the right hand side, the white bar chart has started to "climb the wall" - it finishes with plenty of white tones showing. This is a sign that the highlights have blown out, and lost all detail - you should be able to see areas of pure white somewhere in the image. Is that correct? Yes - some of the petal highlights are pure white.

Using the histogram to check the exposure

If the histogram had looked like the following diagram, then you would know that the exposure the camera had picked was wrong. Because you can look at the histogram, see that the whites fall short of the right hand side of the chart, and then look at the scene and realise that you *should* have pure whites. You would deduce the camera has got the exposure wrong and you can correct it, in this case by increasing the exposure.

This histogram represents an underexposed image, like this one:

A recap

1. The camera's auto modes and LCD sometimes get the exposure wrong

2. Your eye/brain also sometimes gets things wrong

3. The histogram never gets anything wrong

4. You can see whether the exposure is correct by checking if the histogram looks like it should

5. If the histogram is not how it should be, you can compensate for the camera's mistake by changing aperture, shutter speed or ISO

Well done for getting this far. Have a break, come back in 10 minutes.

The last step, compensating for the camera's mistakes, is the easy part. I'll cover that right at the end of the chapter, and you will be practising it for your homework. Before then, just check you understand histograms by having a go at this quiz. The image is on the left. Pick which of the 4 histograms represents the image. Answers and explanations on the following page.

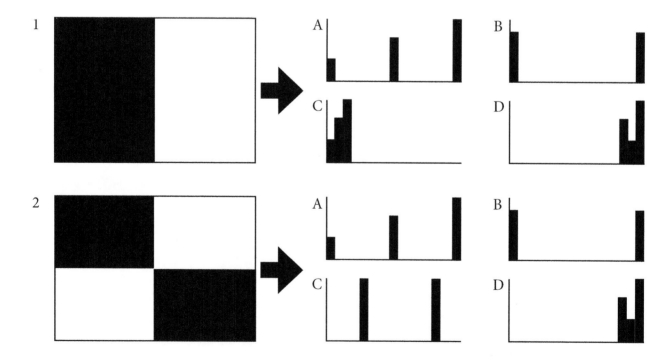

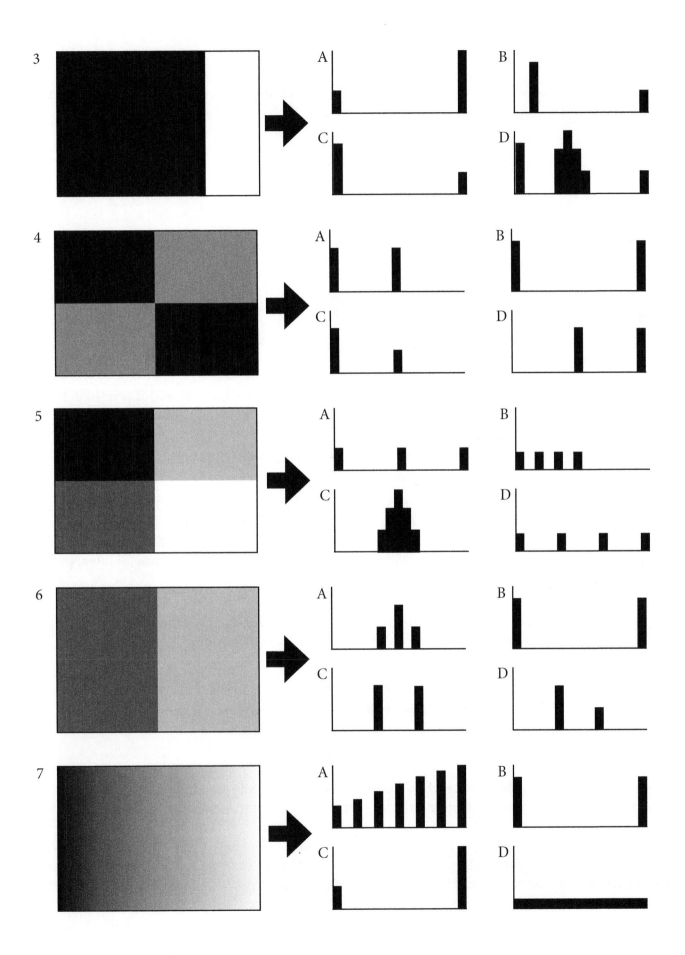

Answers

1: B. The image is half black, half white so you are looking for a histogram with just black and white, nothing else, and the same amount of black and white.

2: B. The image is still half black, half white. The answer is the same. It doesn't matter where in the image the pixels are - the camera just counts them up and plots them on the chart.

3: C. The image is 3/4 black and 1/4 white. The answer has to have all black, and all white with nothing in between, and the black needs to be more than the white.

4: A. The image is half black and half mid grey. The histogram should have 2 bars the same height, one at the black end and one in the middle.

5: D. The image has 2 shades of grey, plus black, plus white. You are looking for a histogram with 4 equal bars, spread across the range from pure black to pure white.

6: C. Half and half but with 2 shades of grey. The histogram should have no pure white or pure black, and the bars should be the same height.

7: D. There are equal amounts of every shade, from black all the way to white. The histogram should be even height and across the whole spectrum.

How to correct exposure quickly - Exposure Compensation

The camera will either have under exposed or over exposed; those are the only 2 things to fix. You either switch to Manual mode and compensate with more/less aperture, shutter speed or ISO, or you can use the exposure compensation function. This function lets you dial in between 1/3 and 2 or more full stops of compensation (depending on your camera) without having to fiddle about with aperture, shutter speed or ISO settings.

This section is optional, but if you're interested, find out how to use exposure compensation from your camera manual. It is probably a dial on the top of your camera. In the viewfinder, look for a scale that looks a bit like this:

⁻3 .. 2 .. 1 .. 0 .. 1 .. 2 .. 3⁺

∎

The scale shows you what's happening when you move the dial. The indicator underneath will move left or right as you dial in plus or minus exposure compensation. So if the histogram showed a slightly underexposed image, you could dial in +1 stop of exposure compensation to let more light in, and the camera will increase the aperture by 1 stop (or the shutter speed, or the ISO - it depends on your camera and the mode you are using). Check your manual to see exactly what your camera will change. You have less control over the exact settings than if you are on Manual mode, but this is a very quick and easy way to get the correct exposure without having to look away from the viewfinder.

Homework - histograms in action

This has been a long, detailed chapter. The concepts are all intermediate to advanced level photography, so if there were sections you didn't understand, that's absolutely fine. If you want to move straight on to the next Part, go right ahead, but bookmark this chapter to come back to in a month or so.

The homework for this chapter is to spend a day with the histogram turned on in your viewfinder, and to check it before you take every photograph. If it looks wrong, then use either Manual mode or exposure compensation to correct the exposure.

1. Start by taking a photograph of a piece of white paper again (not on Manual mode). The camera will assume it is grey, so the histogram should look something like this:

2. You know the paper is white, so you know the histogram should look like this:

3. Use exposure compensation or Manual mode to increase the exposure until the histogram moves all the way to the right. You can watch it move in the viewfinder, if you have it switched on.

4. Now try other subjects, indoors and out, and just pay attention to what the histogram is doing compared to what you think it should be doing.

Converting colour to black and white in your head

You need to be able to estimate how the colours in front of you will convert to greyscale tones. Some things are easy, like dark browns or pale blues. But mid tone colours are harder to place.

You don't need to be too precise. Just look for bright, light tones (any colour) and estimate how much of the image they occupy. Do the same for dark tones. Check whether there are any pure blacks and pure whites, and then look at the histogram to see if it is approximately correct.

Stick one of your homework photos here:

In my own words...

What do I understand now that I didn't before, about metering and histograms?
What do I not really understand, and what is still entirely baffling?

_____

_____

_____

_____

_____

_____

Checklist for Chapter 6

☐ I understand that because the camera assumes everything should be a mid-grey tone, it often under or over exposes photographs

☐ I know that I can't rely on my camera's LCD to check if an image is correctly exposed because the brightness settings might be misleading

☐ I know that I can't rely on my eye/brain combination to tell me how dark or light a scene is because my eyes get used to very dark or very bright situations and my brain tells me they are neither dark nor bright

☐ I know that the histogram never lies

☐ I have worked out how to switch the histogram on in my viewfinder or on my LCD

☐ I have had a go at the quiz, but understand it's not important how many I got right: the important thing is that I read through the answers and explanations

☐ I have done the homework

This is another complex chapter. You don't need to understand everything before you move on. Just be aware of the concepts of metering and histograms, and then come back later in the year to read it through again.

End of Part 1 - test yourself

Consolidate your knowledge by taking these photos:

- ☐ shot with my maximum aperture (biggest hole, smallest number)
- ☐ shot with my minimum aperture (smallest hole, biggest number)
- ☐ shot at f8
- ☐ shutter speed of 1 second
- ☐ shutter speed of 1/1000th second
- ☐ shot with my largest ISO
- ☐ small depth of field
- ☐ large depth of field
- ☐ creative camera shake
- ☐ subject in focus, background blurred
- ☐ background in focus, subject blurred
- ☐ everything in focus
- ☐ moving subject frozen
- ☐ moving subject blurred
- ☐ shot at minimum focus distance and maximum aperture
- ☐ shot at minimum focus distance and minimum aperture

End of Part 1 projects

These are 2 bigger projects, which will ensure you understand all the controls on your camera, and how to expose correctly:

PROJECT 1: depth of field study

Set up a chess board and pieces (or a collection of similar sized things, in a line that starts near the camera and ends farther away from the camera - not a line that starts to the left and finishes on the right). Take a series of images using each of your apertures in turn. Focus on the same chess piece each time (one in the middle), and see what happens to the depth of field.

PROJECT 2: white on white study

Take a photo of something white, on a white background. Take care to get the exposure correct, so the image doesn't turn out grey. Keep enough detail in the shadows that you can see what the subject is.

Don't forget to join the Facebook group (go to AYearWithMyCamera.com/join-facebook) to ask questions, share your photos (if you want to) and meet other people doing the course. If you are on Instagram, use the hashtag #AYearWithMyCamera to share your photos.

PART 2: COMPOSITION

Composition techniques are the tools of the trade for a photographer - the building blocks of every photograph that you will use to create the image you can see in your head.

IT HAD LONG SINCE COME TO MY ATTENTION THAT PEOPLE OF ACCOMPLISHMENT RARELY SAT BACK AND LET THINGS HAPPEN TO THEM. THEY WENT OUT AND HAPPENED TO THINGS.

~ LEONARDO DA VINCI

7: Subject, Background, Foreground

The 3 key elements of any image

Before you can begin to place the 3 key elements where you want them, you will need to understand what they are and the effect they will have on your viewer's experience. The principles in Part 2 don't just apply to photographs. Look at any work of art or skilful piece of graphic design, and you'll see the creator's hand guiding you through the image.

In this chapter

Every image starts with 3 key elements: a subject, a background and a foreground. As the photographer it is your job to decide how each element should interact with the others, and where each will appear in the frame.

You might decide to exclude one element altogether, place your subject so it doesn't overlap with other elements, or reduce the background to a minimum. Each of these decisions, and all the other choices you make surrounding these 3 elements, should be a conscious decision, not an accident.

The balance between these 3 elements should be the first decision you make. Ultimately this will become an almost unconscious process, but to begin with you should take deliberate steps to identify what the subject, background and foreground will be in each image you make.

The balance between the 3 elements

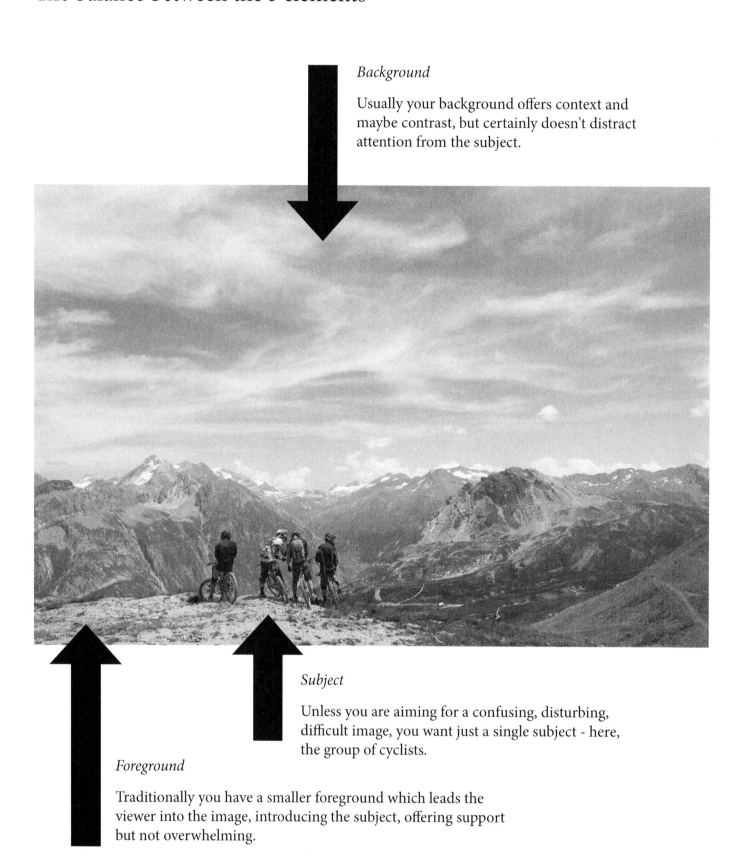

Background

Usually your background offers context and maybe contrast, but certainly doesn't distract attention from the subject.

Subject

Unless you are aiming for a confusing, disturbing, difficult image, you want just a single subject - here, the group of cyclists.

Foreground

Traditionally you have a smaller foreground which leads the viewer into the image, introducing the subject, offering support but not overwhelming.

Images that are out of balance

Too much foreground

The road above adds nothing to the image, which should be framed more tightly, like this:

2 subjects

The eye keeps jumping between the cairn and the buildings. Sometimes a strong foreground can work, but not if it fights the subject for prominence.

Washed out background

The sky here would have been a great background if it had been blue with fluffy clouds. But a washed out grey sky that fades to white adds nothing at all.

Alternatives

The usual balance between the 3 elements that I've outlined isn't the only way to compose a photograph. Sometimes you might want no background or foreground at all, and you fill the frame just with your subject. Landscape photographers often make the foreground the subject. And if you are creating an atonal, disturbing image you'd use many subjects to keep your viewer's eye jumping all around the frame.

As with all established guidelines though, learn the basics first before you start to break the rules.

Using viewpoint to change the balance between the 3 elements

Your point of view is the first, and possibly only, technique you need to change the balance between foreground, subject and background.

Without even moving your feet you can drastically change each element just by moving the camera higher or lower:

If you now allow yourself to walk around your subject, an infinite number of foreground-subject-background combinations will open up:

Homework

Create these photographs, using only a change in viewpoint between images (no changing lenses). You should be able to do this with your phone camera.

- ☐ mostly subject

- ☐ mostly foreground

- ☐ mostly background

- ☐ no subject (this is tricky - try for just more than 1 subject if you get stuck)

- ☐ no foreground

- ☐ no background

- ☐ a pleasing balance between subject, background and foreground

---

Your job as the photographer is to pick the balance of foreground, background and subject that you want. You don't just point and shoot any more. You think, visualise, test and repeat until you have the image you can see in your head.

Use any subject; it can be indoor or out, flash or no flash, whatever you fancy.

The key thing in this chapter is to move your camera. Try shooting from underneath or directly above if you need to. Move closer and further away, and change the angle of the camera.

Don't worry about aperture, shutter speed, ISO and exposure if you want a break from the technicals. For this lesson I just want you to start moving with your camera.

Checklist for Chapter 7

☐ I understand that an image has 3 elements: a background, a foreground and a subject

☐ I know that I can choose to exclude one or more elements from my final image, but it must be a conscious decision and not an accident

☐ I understand the importance of having a single subject, unless my image is intended to be disturbing for the viewer

☐ I will be careful not to include too much foreground in my images

☐ I will check my skies from now on, and I will not include a big expanse of blown-out white sky

☐ I know that I can make a huge difference to the balance of elements in my image just by moving my viewpoint, sometimes only by a centimetre

☐ I have done the homework

Stick your homework photos here:

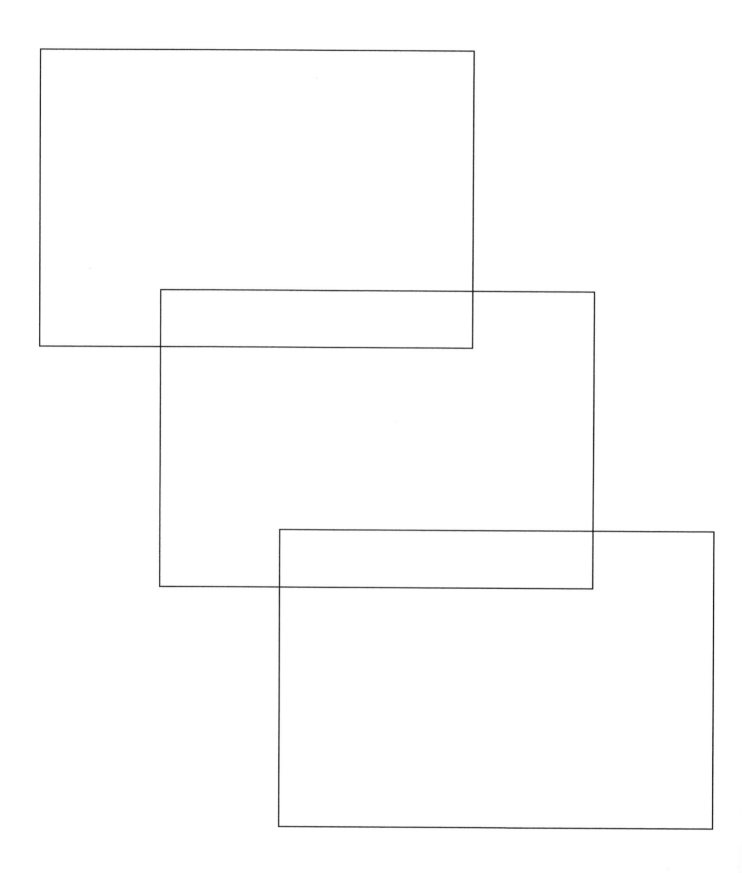

LUCK IS WHAT HAPPENS WHEN PREPARATION MEETS OPPORTUNITY

~ ATTRIBUTED TO SENECA THE YOUNGER

8: Single focal point

One subject for each image - no more, no less

Strong photographs have just one subject that the viewer can pick out immediately. Part of the skill of the photographer is to eliminate unnecessary and distracting elements from the photograph, and that includes anything that will compete with your single subject for attention.

In this chapter

When someone looks at your photograph, their eye will be searching out something to rest on. If they can't find anything - if they have to keep jumping from one thing to another - they will be impatient, annoyed, anxious, unsettled, and disturbed. If that's what you want them to feel, then you've taken a great photograph.

If not, make it your mission to help the viewer of your photograph by giving them a single focal point - one subject - to find and rest their eyes on.

You should use the viewpoint techniques from the last chapter to move your subject within the frame until you have a strong balance between subject, background and foreground. And then you can use one or more of the composition ideas from this chapter to draw further attention to your subject and create strong, eyecatching images.

You need to make it clear that the single focal point is not the foreground, nor the background - it is the subject of the photograph and the reason the viewer is looking at the image.

Composition techniques to try

Once you have made sure you have just one subject, there are a few composition techniques you can use to help draw the viewer's eye to it, and establish its authority as the single focal point.

1. Size in relation to other elements

Possibly the most obvious, but if your subject takes up more space in the frame than competing subjects, it will stand out as the main point of interest.

Look at the 2 girls at the table in the photo opposite. Although there are plenty of other people in the photo, it's clear that they are the subject because of their size relative to the others.

2. Position in the frame

Use your feet to move around your subject until it is placed where you want it in the frame. Usually you want your subject towards the front of the frame (so don't have too much foreground), or you want it deliberately positioned in a strong place.

In the image of the girls opposite, they are deliberately placed at the front of the frame, and very slightly off centre to avoid a perfectly symmetrical image. Asymmetry creates tension and interest. Symmetry is much more static.

For a strong subject placement, try using the rule of thirds. This means putting your subject on one of the 4 imaginary lines that divide the frame into 3 sections, vertically and horizontally. And for an even stronger image, place it on one of the intersections:

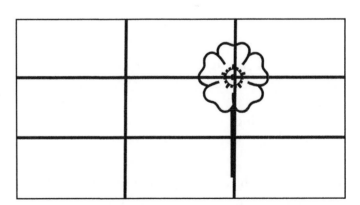

3. Contrast with the background

To make your subject stand out from the background, use contrast. In the image on the previous page, the girls are silhouetted and so contrast starkly with the lighter toned pavement.

Contrasts you can try include:

- ▶ colour
- ▶ texture
- ▶ tone
- ▶ light

4. Separation from other elements

As well as keeping the subject separate from the background, you should also avoid letting other elements in the image overlap with the subject (unless it's done deliberately). In the image of the courtyard, the girls don't overlap with the buildings at the back, or with any of the other tables and chairs.

Avoid letting the subject touch or overlap with other elements, unless you definitely want that effect.

5. Point to the subject

This is a not-so-subtle technique to use other elements in the frame to draw attention to the subject. There are 2 commonly used versions:

- ▶ framing
- ▶ leading lines

To frame the subject, simply shoot through a natural frame and position the subject beyond.

Leading lines are typically things like footpaths or fences that draw the eye through the frame towards the subject.

Homework

Make these photos. Just pick one or two for now if you don't have time to work through them all, but come back to them when you have a chance.

- ☐ just one subject, with no competing subjects

- ☐ subject stands out because of its size in relation to all the other elements

- ☐ subject placed on one of the rule of thirds lines

- ☐ subject is a different colour to the background

- ☐ background is blurred (use the large aperture method described in chapter 2)

- ☐ subject is carefully placed to avoid touching any other elements in the frame

- ☐ subject is framed by something else within the photo

- ☐ leading lines draw the eye to the subject

Most important things to remember for beginners:

1. Don't let the subject get lost in the background

2. Don't let the foreground take up so much space in the frame that the subject gets lost in comparison

3. Have just one subject, and keep competing subjects either out of the frame or smaller in comparison

Stick your 2 best homework photos here:

Checklist for Chapter 8

☐ I understand that unless I am creating a disturbing, atonal image, I should have just one, clear focal point

☐ I know from the previous chapter that I should use viewpoint to change the position of the subject in relation to the other elements in the image

☐ I know that I can also draw attention to my subject using composition techniques including: size of image, position in the frame, contrast with the background, separation from other elements, and "pointing" to the subject using framing and leading lines

☐ I have done at least 2 of the homework photos

VISION WITHOUT ACTION IS DAYDREAM. ACTION WITHOUT VISION IS NIGHTMARE.

~ JAPANESE PROVERB

9: Design principles

Being deliberate about what's in the frame

Ansel Adams, possibly the greatest landscape photographer ever, said, "You don't take a photograph, you make it.". To turn a snapshot into a photograph you need to be very deliberate about everything you include in the frame, and where you put it.

In this chapter

There are plenty of design principles that photographers can borrow in their quest for an aesthetically pleasing photograph. In this chapter I outline just 6 that you can call upon when you are composing your photographs.

You won't need to use them all in a single image, but combined with the techniques from the previous 2 chapters: one or two used carefully will take your photography to an advanced level.

Thinking about the whole frame

In the last two chapters you've been looking at using viewpoint to change the balance between subject, foreground and background, and also concentrating on having a single focal point in your image.

In this chapter I'm going to run through 6 composition principles that photographers borrow from graphic designers to create aesthetically pleasing images (pleasing to the Western design aesthetic, at least). They all need you to take a step back and think about the whole frame again.

1. Odd numbers

It's a basic principle of human behaviour that we prefer odd numbers. Things grouped in 3s or 5s are more pleasing than 2s or 4s. It's the same idea that lies behind the rule of thirds in the last chapter - humans prefer slight asymmetry.

If you compose in 2s and 4s you'll find your images are static and dull. 3s and 5s adds a bit of tension and movement.

2. Fill the frame

Do away with foreground and background altogether, and fill the frame with your subject. This can make for an intense, abstract photo, so use sparingly.

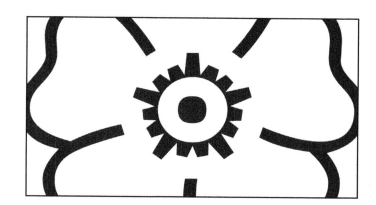

3. Symmetry

No real explanation needed - we love symmetry in a photo. Don't forget it can go diagonally as well as horizontally/vertically.

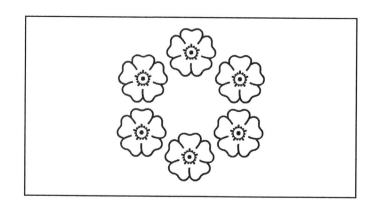

4. Diagonals

Much like the rule of thirds and the odd numbers technique, using diagonals will add tension and interest to your photograph. Using straight lines will create static, dull images.

5. Repetition

Humans like things that follow a pattern, where we can predict what will happen next.

6. Negative space

This is an extension of the technique of isolating the subject from other elements in the frame, covered in the last chapter. The empty space around your subject is called negative space, or white space. You can view it as an element to itself.

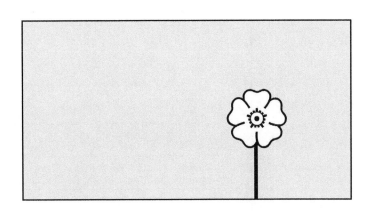

Things to remember:

1. Think about your subject, the foreground, and the background

2. It should be clear what your subject is - have one focal point with no distractions or competing subjects

3. Move the camera up and down, and walk around your subject, until you have the subject where you want it in the frame, balanced as you want it with the background and the foreground

4. Use techniques like the rule of thirds and leading lines to draw attention to your subject

5. Use techniques borrowed from the design world (symmetry, odd numbers) as you look at the whole frame

6. Don't try and do everything in the same image - if you can remember just one thing to start off with that will be fine

In my own words...

Thinking back over everything you've read and practised so far in Part 2, what has stood out for you? What do you know now that you didn't when you started?

_____

_____

_____

_____

_____

_____

_____

Homework

Make these photos. Just pick one or two for now if you don't have time to work through them all, but come back to them when you have a chance.

☐ arrange your subject in a group of 3 or 5, and check that in the final image the group is cohesive enough to become a single subject rather than 3 or 5 separate objects

☐ fill the frame with your subject - no background and no foreground

☐ create a symmetrical image

☐ find natural diagonals and use them to make a dynamic, interesting image

☐ use repetition in an image, and try to avoid it becoming static

☐ use negative space to create a strong image

Too much? 3 arches, symmetry, repetition, leading lines, framing, and diagonals, all in the same image.

Stick your 2 best homework photos here:

Checklist for Chapter 9

☐ I haven't forgotten from the previous chapters that I should have a single focal point, deliberately placed in the frame to balance the background and the foreground, and that I can use composition techniques like size and the rule of thirds to draw attention to it

☐ I understand that Western design aesthetic includes universally applicable principles that can be applied to photography, including symmetry, repetition and diagonals

☐ Once I've composed my photograph I'll remember to check around the frame for distractions, and to consider how the image works as a whole

☐ I've completed at least one of the homework projects

ART IS NOT WHAT YOU SEE BUT WHAT YOU MAKE OTHERS SEE

~ EDGAR DEGAS

10: Advanced composition

Bringing it all together

Why are you taking photographs?

No really - why?

Take a couple of minutes to think about it.

In this chapter

When you take a photograph, what are you trying to say, and who are you trying to say it to?

We all take photographs for different reasons.

To take a photo we're proud of, to win a competition, to make a walk more interesting, or because we said we'd take a photo every day for a year. Maybe it's to show off, to hang on the wall, or because we want to preserve our children or grandchildren's childhood. It might be just to learn how to use the camera, or to be popular on Instagram.

Whatever your reason, even if it's just because you want to finish this chapter's homework, someone will look at your image. It might just be you having

a quick glance on the back of the camera before you delete it. But hopefully it will make it out into the world and be seen by other people.

The point is - you have a chance to speak to the person looking at your photograph. You owe it to yourself and to that person to think about what you want to say before you press the shutter.

This chapter is a bit more philosophical than the previous ones, but it's a critical step on your path to becoming a great photographer. Why are you taking the photograph, and how will you communicate with your viewer?

Composition is the language of photography

Think of your composition as the language you use to speak to your viewer. Your camera might be your voice, and the quality of light (which we'll start looking at in the next chapter) the tone of your voice - but the backbone of your photograph is the composition, the common language that you both understand.

Where do you put everything in the frame?

What do you leave out?

How do all the elements relate to each other?

How can you use these principles to reduce a 3 dimensional scene to a 2 dimensional representation that echoes the finished image you see in your head?

Becoming fluent

Just as you learn any language, you first learn some vocabulary and some grammar. Everything you've learnt so far in Part 2 is your vocabulary - the individual words of the language of photography.

In this chapter you will learn some grammar; how do you combine words (the basic composition techniques) to communicate more complex ideas and emotions? What advanced techniques can you use to add layers, nuance and depth of meaning to your images?

Don't forget - one day soon you'll take a photograph where you have unconsciously placed the subject where you want it, knelt down to get a better viewpoint and used a shallow depth of field to blur out the background. You'll have considered some advanced techniques, and your camera will stop being a barrier between you and your finished image, but rather the tool that you're completely comfortable with, that gives voice to your ideas. At this point you have become fluent.

Advanced composition techniques

In this chapter I want you to look at some bigger picture composition ideas. In previous chapters you've looked in isolation at techniques like the rule of thirds, using symmetry, having a single focal point. In this chapter I want you to think deeply about why you take photographs generally, why

you are taking the particular photograph you are about to take, and how you can use the language of composition to speak to your viewer.

Start here (there is no right answer):

In my own words...

Why do I take photographs?

_____

_____

_____

Advanced techniques

You've learnt a lot of composition vocabulary in the last 3 chapters. Here are a couple of grammar points you can bear in mind when you're assembling your photographs.

1. Visual weight

This extends the principles of having a single focal point, and thinking about the balance between subject, foreground and background.

How much of the viewer's attention does each element of the photograph claim?

The most obvious attention seeker is the biggest thing in the frame, but there are other things to consider. All of these things are said to have visual weight:

- faces will automatically draw the viewer's eye, no matter how small (and even if they are not actually faces, just clouds or rocks that look like a face)

- anything red will attract a disproportionate amount of attention

- specular highlights (white spots or burnt out areas) will also draw attention

- anything that contrasts with the rest of the frame will stand out - not just colour, but things like a large expanse of shadow next to a more textured subject, or a bird flying out of the frame when all the others are flying in

How much of the viewer's attention does each element of your photograph claim?

93

2. What's out of frame?

Although the viewer can only see what you've included in the frame, you can suggest action out of the frame to add to the composition. This is usually done when things are clearly incomplete - a parent holding out a hand for an absent child, someone making eye contact with another person out of the frame, or when you only include part of your subject.

3. What's leaving the frame?

Be very, very careful about each edge of your image. What's leaving the frame, and where is it leaving? Be intentional.

4. What's overlapping?

We looked at this in chapter 8, in relation to the subject touching or overlapping with other elements in the frame. But the same principle applies to everything in the image, subject or not.

Give elements of your image breathing space. Don't let them overlap with each other unless that's what you want. You need to train your eye to spot when an image could be improved if elements were separated. Often you only need to move the camera a couple of inches. This is a critical skill to develop for landscape and still life photographers especially.

Homework

Take a photograph where you communicate something to your viewer. Be deliberate about your subject, background and foreground. Think about where to place everything in the frame. Consider what to include and what to leave out. Can you use any design principles to help you get your message across?

You can do anything you like, but if you need a starting place, try taking one of these photographs:

melancholy	abundant
balanced	silent
tired	timeless
expectant	persistent
happy	distorted
impatient	true
choices	impossible
isolation	old
sinister	complete

What route through the frame does the viewer's eye take? Where does it stop? Where does it leave? Where does it get distracted?

Stick your homework photo here:

In my own words...

What I was trying to say with this image, and my thoughts on this exercise:

_____

_____

_____

_____

_____

_____

Checklist for Chapter 10

☐ I've thought carefully about all the reasons I take photographs

☐ I understand that photographs that speak to the viewer don't just happen by accident, but that I'll need to think and plan

☐ I won't forget Ansel Adams' saying that you don't take a photograph, you make it

☐ I understand the more advanced composition techniques described in this chapter, and I know not to use them all in the same image

☐ I've completed at least one of the homework projects

End of Part 2 - test yourself

Consolidate your knowledge by taking these photos:

- ☐ mostly foreground

- ☐ no background at all

- ☐ 1 subject, 12 viewpoints

- ☐ make the sky the subject

- ☐ background separation (make sure the subject is clearly separate from the background)

- ☐ rule of thirds

- ☐ single focal point

- ☐ a static image

- ☐ a dynamic image

- ☐ an image that leaves questions unanswered

- ☐ give too much visual weight to the background

- ☐ echo something from the subject in the background (shape, colour, texture)

- ☐ try and recreate a famous painting with your camera

- ☐ an image where subject, background and foreground each take up exactly 1/3 of the frame

- ☐ tell a story in 1 image

End of Part 2 project

Composition techniques are the tools you have beyond the camera to turn your vision into a photograph. The more familiar you are with the effect each technique has on the final image, the easier it will be to turn the images you can see in your head into reality.

PROJECT: turning vision into reality

Use the following 5 prompts as the starting point for 5 images. Read through Part 2 again, and decide which composition techniques will best help you achieve the vision you have for each image you want to take. When you are taking your photographs, work on one image at a time, and try different techniques until you arrive at a strong image.

1: safe

2: Once upon a time...

3: confused

4: set in stone

5: step by step

If you want to stretch yourself, pick any of the quotes from the end of the chapters in this book and use that as a starting point for a photo.

Share in the Facebook group, if you've joined (not too late to join: AYearWithMyCamera.com/join-facebook), and on Instagram with the #AYearWithMyCamera hashtag.

Technical revision

Don't forget what you learnt in Part 1. Can you still take these photos?

☐ subject in focus, background blurred

☐ large depth of field

☐ shot at your closest focussing distance

☐ moving subject frozen

☐ 1 second exposure

☐ use the histogram to get the correct exposure when you take a photograph of a piece of white paper

☐ take a photo on auto, write down settings, change the aperture and shutter speed but keep the exposure the same

PART 3: LIGHT

In the first part of this book you learnt how to use your camera simply to control the amount of light hitting the sensor.

In the second part you didn't worry so much about light - we were looking at using composition to control where you placed all the elements in your image.

In this part of the course I'll show you how light is an element of your image all to itself.

KNOWING IS NOT ENOUGH;
WE MUST APPLY. WILLING IS
NOT ENOUGH; WE MUST DO.

~ JOHAN WOLFGANG VON GOETHE

11: Direction of light

Light is a separate element of your photograph

Photography means, "painting with light". When you are taking a photograph, light is your raw material, your unmoulded clay, your box of paints.

In this chapter

You are used, by now, to look for the subject, the foreground and the background of each photograph you take. In this chapter I want you to start looking for the light in each image as well.

Light is what will bring your photograph alive, and you should take control of it - don't leave its influence to chance.

There are 2 aspects of the light you need to look for: the direction and the quality. Each will affect your photograph, and each can be controlled. In this chapter we'll look at direction, and in the next, quality.

The direction of light, and the effect it has on your image

There are 6 main directions light can come from:

- top down
- directly in front
- from one side

- bottom up
- directly behind
- from the other side

There are variations and subtleties (eg. from the top but slightly to one side), but for this chapter, just think about these 6 directions.

top down

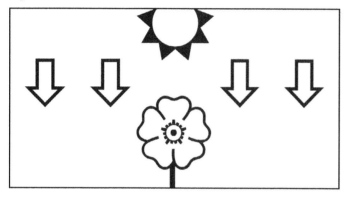

bottom up

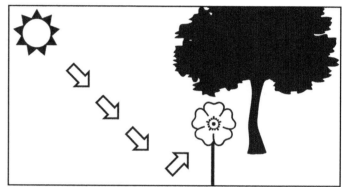

directly in front

directly behind

from one side

from the other side

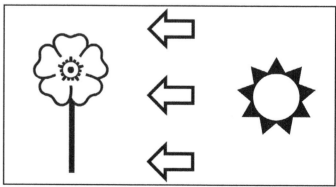

Top down light

Typically this is what you get when you shoot outdoors at midday. The sun is overhead and, unless it is behind a cloud, you will get bright, harsh, contrasty light.

Look out for hard shadows and washed-out colours.

Bottom up light

Humans are used to the main light coming from somewhere on an arc that starts on one side of the horizon, goes up above, and comes down the other side. The sun's path, in other words. Anything that deviates from this looks wrong and unnatural. Horror films are shot with the light coming from below the baddie's face to make them look sinister. Avoid this for day to day images.

Front light

Imagine you are the subject and the sun is blazing straight into your face. What do you do? Squint. That's the first downside to front lighting. Another is that, like top lighting, it tends to wash out colours and gives a very flat feeling with no depth. Lastly, it gets rid of all texture by blasting the shadows to nothing. Good, if you want to eliminate wrinkles; not so good if you want an interesting landscape.

Back light

The old fashioned advice used to be, "never shoot into the sun". Ignore that advice from now on. Back lighting is one of my favourites - it creates depth, interest, and you'll often get a gorgeous rim light around your subject to help pop it out from the background. It fools the camera's auto exposure though, so if you're not on Manual mode, make a note that you'll need to *overexpose by 1-2 stops.*

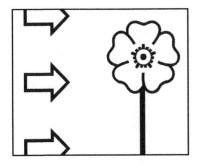

Side light

Side light brings out all the texture in your subject by creating shadows right across the image. It's the landscape photographer's preferred lighting set up, and also adds depth and interest to still life and character portraits.

Homework

Pick any subject, something that you can move around, and light it in each of the 6 ways described in this chapter:

- from above

- from below

- from the front

- from the back

- from the left

- from the right

Try the homework inside, using artificial light, and also outside, using daylight.

For the indoor version you can use any kind of light - a desklight, a torch, the light on your phone.

Make sure your flash is turned off, otherwise all your images will be front-lit. If your camera is struggling to take photos on P or Auto modes, it may be because it is too dark. Go back to the chapters in Part 1, and put your camera on shutter priority mode. Choose a shutter speed of 1/60th or 1/125th, and let the camera pick the aperture. Use a high ISO if it's still struggling - as high as you need to go.

You should notice that it's easier to make all 6 photos indoors, because you can move the light around your subject. But once you head outside you will need to move yourself all around the subject to change the position of the light in relation to your subject. And you might not be able to finish all the photos at the same time - you might need to come back later when the sun has changed position.

If you're working with short days, or cloudy weather, bookmark the outdoors homework to come back to when you have a sunny day.

	Indoors		*Outdoors*
	☐ above		☐ above
	☐ below		☐ below
	☐ front		☐ front
	☐ back		☐ back
	☐ left		☐ left
	☐ right		☐ right

Things to remember:

1. Imagine the light is a separate element that you need to consider for each photograph you take

2. The direction the light is coming from will influence the feel of your photograph

3. You can control the direction of the light by either moving the light, or moving yourself

Stick your homework photos here:

Checklist for Chapter 11

☐ I will look on light as an element all to itself in each photograph I take from now on

☐ I understand that light falls on a subject from a definite direction, even on a cloudy day

☐ I understand that I can control the direction of light, either by moving the light or by moving myself

☐ I've made a start on the homework, even if I've not finished all of it

In my own words...

Why is the direction of light important?

_____

_____

_____

_____

_____

_____

TAKING A NEW STEP, UTTERING
A NEW WORD, IS WHAT PEOPLE
FEAR MOST.

~ FYODOR DOSTOYEVSKY

12: Quality of light

How often do you look at the shadows?

The biggest secret that pro photographers never share is that it's the shadows that make the photograph, not the light itself.

In this chapter

I touched on shadows in the last chapter, and you should have noticed that as you move the direction the light is coming from, so the shadows move across your photograph.

But there is much, much more to a good shadow than just the way it falls.

Your shadows are what gives your image depth, character, form and life. And once again, as the photographer, you need to take control of the shadows.

You might have heard people describe the quality of light as hard or soft before. It's more accurate to describe the *shadows* as hard or soft, because that's what we see in the final image.

Either way, what matters is that hard light gives hard shadows, and soft light gives soft shadows. In this chapter you'll learn first, to spot hard and soft shadows, second to decide which kind you want, and third, how to create them.

Hard shadows and soft shadows

Take a moment to look around where you are right now. What kind of shadows can you see? How many have hard edges, and can you see any with soft edges?

Are there any that are so soft that you can't really tell where they begin and end?

hard shadow

soft shadow

Which shadows do you want?

You need to go back to the question you asked in Chapter 10 - why are you taking this photograph? You will use the quality of shadows to help you create the image you want. Hard shadows typically give high contrast, graphic, aggressive images. Soft shadows give gentler, more subtle images. There's no right answer to the question of which is the best shadow type. For a character portrait you might want harder shadows than for a flattering portrait. Landscapes typically have more depth and atmosphere with longer, softer shadows. Soft shadows bring out the shape and form of a still life in a way that hard shadows would eliminate.

How to create hard and soft shadows

Hard light gives hard shadows. Soft light gives soft shadows.

Technically, the smaller the light source in relation to the subject, the harder the shadows. But you don't need to be puzzling out the inverse square rule to notice what your eyes will tell you.

If you notice that the shadows have hard edges, you can soften them (or "diffuse" them) in one of 2 ways: use a diffuser to break the light up, or put your subject in the shade so the light is now indirect. (A diffuser is simply something translucent like the clouds, a piece of tracing paper, or a sheet. Anything that still lets light through, but softens the shadows.)

Homework

Go on a shadow safari. Spend the day, or the weekend, collecting different types of shadow. Start with naturally occuring ones, and then try creating your own. Use both natural and artificial light, and try different diffusers.

Don't forget to turn your flash off, unless you're deliberately using flash as your light source.

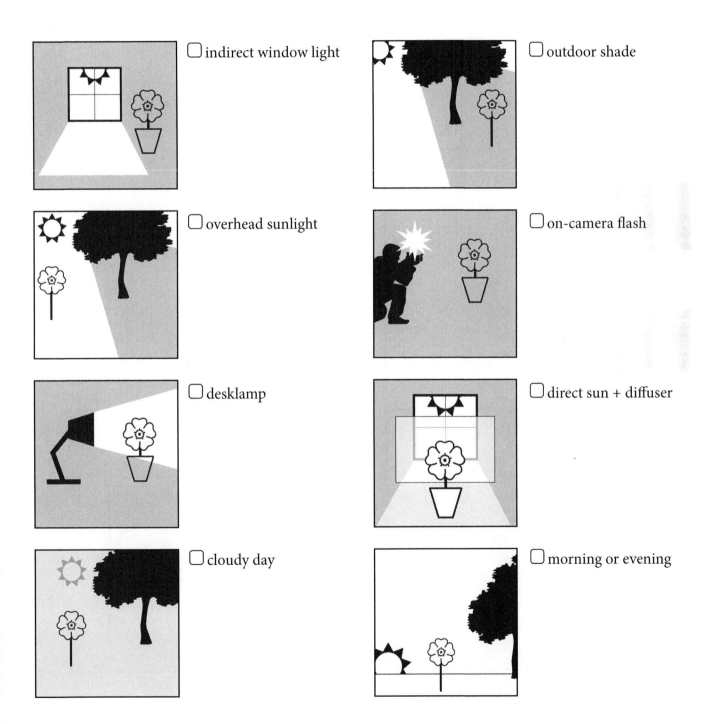

☐ indirect window light

☐ outdoor shade

☐ overhead sunlight

☐ on-camera flash

☐ desklamp

☐ direct sun + diffuser

☐ cloudy day

☐ morning or evening

Stick your homework photos here:

Checklist for Chapter 12

☐ I understand hard (or "direct") light gives hard shadows, and soft (or "indirect") light gives soft shadows

☐ I understand that the quality of the light, and therefore the shadows, affects the tone of my final image

☐ I know that one kind of light is not better than any other - the important thing is how I want my image to look

☐ I know that I can control the softness of the light by using diffusers, or by moving my subject out of direct light and into indirect light (ie. into the shade)

☐ I know that if I am using direct light the shadows will be harder than if I'm using indirect light

☐ I've made a start on the homework, even if I've not finished all of it

BEGIN, BE BOLD AND VENTURE TO BE WISE

~ HORACE

13: Colour of light

Your eyes will always try to deceive you

Your eyes work in tandem with your brain to see the world and interpret it for you. This is mostly good, except when you need to be utterly objective. The need for objectivity is critical when it comes to assessing the colour of light in your image.

In this chapter

All light sources have a temperature which translates to a colour cast (eg. sunlight is warm/yellow, shade is cool/blue). So if you take the same photograph lit first by sunlight and then in the shade, it will have a slightly different colour cast in each image - yellow in the first, and blue in the second.

This often doesn't matter, and in fact you can use the warm/cool tint to add atmosphere to your photograph. But if your subject is white, or the colour cast is very strong, your images can start to look wrong.

There are 2 ways to fix a colour cast, but only a handful of times you will need to do it. The most common situation is when you are shooting indoors.

Almost all photographs taken indoors have a slight yellow colour cast to them which you probably don't notice, because your brain compensates for you. It interprets the image and tells you that what *should* be a white piece of paper *is* white, even if in fact it is yellow. But your indoor photos will start to look 100% more professional if you get rid of the yellow tint.

In this chapter I'll explain the 2 ways to fix the problem.

COOL

WARM

9000   blue sky

8000

7000   shade

6000   cloud

5000   midday sun

4000   fluorescent

3000   indoor tungsten

2000   sunrise/sunset

1000   candlelight

How to fix colour temperature

1. Get it right in-camera

The chart opposite shows the colour temperature scale for visible light. It starts at 1000 Kelvin for very warm candlelight. It progresses through different times of day and different types of artificial light to finish with 9000 Kelvin for a clear blue sky.

If it's important that your colour temperature is accurate, you can dial in the exact Kelvin measurement. Check your manual for instructions (it may refer to "white balance"). You dial in the temperature you are actually shooting at, so that the camera can adjust the white balance accordingly.

If you can get away with an approximation of the lighting temperature, you can use one of the preset colour temperature settings. Look for the icons listed on the previous page.

The default option will be to use the Auto white balance setting. I leave mine on Auto most of the time, and it's usually good enough. If you do have a go at using the presets or the Manual settings, remember to put it back to Auto when you have finished.

2. Fix it in post processing

Most editing software will have a white balance slider, or a place for you to specify the exact colour temperature. Many also have an eyedropper tool where you can click on any part of the image which is supposed to be white (or grey), and it will take that as the baseline.

I use Lightroom, and the eyedropper tool is in the Develop module, near the top. The free online software Picmonkey has a similar function: go to Picmonkey.com, then choose the neutral picker tool which is under Basic Edits.

Homework

  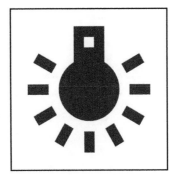

1. Work out how to change the white balance ("WB") on your camera using both the presets, and the actual Kelvin settings (remember to put it back to auto afterwards).

2. On auto WB, take photos that include something white, in at least 3 different lighting conditions - sunlight, shade, indoor lights. Be as objective as you can, and see if the whites are truly white.

3. Put your camera on the tungsten setting. Now take the same 3 photos and see what happens.

4. Dial in a high Kelvin setting, like 7500K, and retake the same 3 photos.

Stick your homework photos here:

Checklist for Chapter 13

☐ I understand that my eyes/brain don't always give me accurate information, and that they might tell me a white piece of paper is white in a photograph even though it actually has a yellow or blue colour cast

☐ I understand that every light source has a colour temperature which, if uncorrected, my camera will record as a colour cast

☐ I know how to correct colour casts in-camera by using the white balance feature on my camera

☐ I know that I can correct colour casts in post processing by using either a white balance tool, or a neutral picker

☐ I know that at the warm end of the Kelvin scale I'll find candlelight, at 1000K

☐ I know that at the cool end of the Kelvin scale I'll find clear blue skies, at 9000K

☐ I know that midday sun is about 5200K

☐ I know that cloudy sky is about 6000K

☐ I've made a start on the homework

OUR DOUBTS ARE TRAITORS, AND MAKE US LOSE THE GOOD WE OFT MIGHT WIN, BY FEARING TO ATTEMPT

~ SHAKESPEARE, MEASURE FOR MEASURE

14: Using 2 lights

Using light to create the image you want

Photography is all about taking control - of your camera, of the composition, and now of the light. Just because the light isn't how you want it to start with, doesn't mean you can't do anything about it.

In this chapter

So far we've assumed you're dealing with a single source of light - the sun, a torch, a desklamp. But you will have more options if you have more than one source of light. The disadvantage of having a strong light coming from a single direction - hard shadows - can be overcome if you have a second light.

Photographers working in studios can set up as many lights as they want. They can angle them, turn them up or down, make them hard or soft. I'm assuming you're just working with natural daylight though, and maybe a flash.

You can get a lot of the benefits available to studio photographers with no need for new kit if you appreciate the fact that a second light source doesn't have to be an entirely new light - it can simply be the original light source, but reflected.

In this chapter I'll explain how to use a reflector as a second light source to create a fill light which will soften hard shadows.

What is a fill light?

If you have one particularly strong light source (the midday sun for example), it will throw correspondingly strong shadows. This results in what's called a high dynamic range ("HDR") in your photograph - you have a very bright side of your image on the side of the sun, and a very dark opposite side.

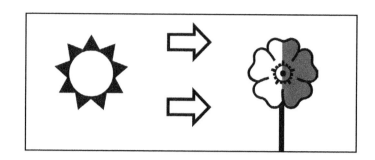

Contrast this with a low dynamic range image which would happen if you shot on a cloudy day - no particularly bright spots, and no very dark shadows.

The problem with an HDR image is that your camera's sensor has a dynamic range which is smaller than the eye's. It can't fit both the darks and the brights in the same image. The result is that you lose all the information at one end of the dynamic range, and end up with blocky black shadows, or blown out highlights.

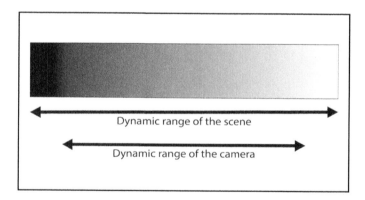

The solution is to reduce the dynamic range (on your subject at least) by reducing the shadows. You do this by shining a second light source into them. The technical term for this is "fill light", but as I explained above, it doesn't have to be an actual light. You can get this effect just by reflecting the sunlight back into the shadows.

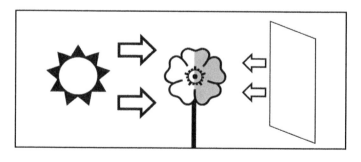

The fill light should never be as strong as the main light. You are not trying to get the effect of 2 spotlights shining on your subject. An effective fill light will not be noticeable.

How to use a reflector

You can buy custom designed reflectors in white, gold and silver. Or you can use anything handy that is reflective. The only reflectors I use regularly are A1 pieces of 5mm foamcore (available from art shops) - they are very light and easy to position. I've also used bedsheets, paper and aluminium foil. On location you can position your subject to take advantage of natural reflectors such as sand or white walls. Here's what to do:

1. Identify the main source of light.

2. Position yourself or your subject where you want to be, in relation to the main light source.

3. The reflector needs to be directly opposite the main light source, and angled towards the shadows that need softening. The reflector needs to be very close.

4. You should be able to see the shadows changing with your naked eye, so move the reflector until you get the effect you want.

How to use fill flash

If your main light source is coming from behind your subject (eg you are shooting into the sun), you can use your on-camera flash instead of a physical reflector.

Be very careful of using too much flash. You should simply be aiming to compensate slightly for the strong directional light coming from behind your subject with a gentle fill light - you are not trying to make your flash the main light source. This is a reasonably advanced technique which I include for completeness, but feel free to skip this information for now. If you are interested in trying it out, look up "fill flash" in your manual.

Homework

An easy one for this chapter: just take 2 photos in conditions where you have a very strong, direct main light (eg. overhead sunlight rather than a cloudy day). Take one photo with no reflector, and one photo with a reflector.

Position your subject so that the main light is either coming top down (so you reflect upwards from the front), or from the side (so you reflect from the other side).

You are aiming to see very strong contrast and hard shadows in the first photo, and softer shadows in the second. I took these images using my iPad case as a reflector. Look at the shadow on the table - in the second image it is lighter grey than the first:

Stick your homework photos here:

Checklist for Chapter 14

☐ I know that HDR stands for High Dynamic Range

☐ I understand that my camera won't be able to keep all the detail in both the shadows and the highlights of an HDR image

☐ I understand that an image taken in strong, direct light will probably have a dynamic range greater than my camera can cope with

☐ I know that I can reduce the dynamic range of an image by softening (brightening) the shadows

☐ I know that using a second light source, even if that is just the main light source reflected, is a technique I can use to soften shadows

☐ I know that using a second light source like this is called a "fill light"

☐ I know that my fill light should not be anywhere near as strong as my main light, and that it shouldn't be noticeable in the final image

☐ I've completed the reflector/no reflector homework

End of Part 3 - test yourself

Consolidate your knowledge by taking these photos:

☐ same subject lit in 6 different ways

☐ contrejour (literally, "against the day" - ie. shot into the light, with the light behind the subject)

☐ hard shadows

☐ soft shadows

☐ no shadows

☐ use a diffuser

☐ use the wrong colour temperature setting for your conditions

☐ 2 colours of light in the same photo

☐ shoot something white in 4 different colour temperatures, and make sure the white stays white in all 4

☐ find a high dynamic range scene and use the histogram to first expose for the highlights and then expose for the shadows

☐ use a mirror as a reflector to create a fill light

☐ use a torch or phone screen light to create a fill light

☐ try using your on-camera flash as a fill light for a back-lit subject

☐ take a photograph where the light (or the shadows) is (are) the subject

End of Part 3 project

PROJECT: Take an image you are proud of

1. Pick a subject that motivates you, something you will enjoy photographing.

2. Consider what you want to say with your image, how you want the subject to be portrayed, and how you want other people to interpret your vision. Write this down.

3. Settings: which is the most important setting for your image - aperture or shutter speed? Start there and build your exposure around it.

4. Composition: start with the background, decide if you need a foreground, and think about how much space your subject will take up in the frame. Where will you position your subject, and will it leave the frame? What viewpoint will you use? What else, if anything, will appear in the frame, and where? Why? Everything has to earn its place.

5. Light: how will you use light to sculpt your subject? How will the light affect the background? Where will you be positioned in relation to the main light source?

6. Take your photograph, review, and change anything you need to change. Refer back to what you wrote down in step 2. Repeat this step as often as you need to.

7. When you have an image you are proud of, print it out and put it on the wall. You don't need to frame it, but it must go on display.

Technical revision

Don't forget what you learnt in Part 1. Can you still take these photos?

☐ blur the background when you are at least 2 metres away from your subject

☐ shot on your smallest aperture

☐ blur a moving subject

☐ 1/4000th shutter speed (or whatever your fastest is)

☐ 3 second exposure (use the "bulb" or "B" setting - look it up in the manual)

☐ use the histogram to get the correct exposure when you take a photograph of a piece of black paper

☐ take a photo on auto, write down settings, then take 4 photos with different aperture/shutter speed/ISO combinations but the same exposure

PART 4: CREATIVITY

So far you've been mainly learning how to use your camera to create the image you can see in your head.

In this part you'll be exploring what that image is in the first place - how can you imagine more exciting, creative and eye-catching photographs that you can go on to take?

STOP A MOMENT, CEASE YOUR WORK, LOOK AROUND YOU

~ LEO TOLSTOY

15: Setting boundaries

Unleashing your creativity

Apart from getting to know your camera better, what's stopping you taking the photos you always dreamed of? Are you dreaming big enough?

In this chapter

Do you despair of ever having an original idea? Do you wish you could do something a bit different with your camera, a bit more personal, a bit more interesting? Well the good news is your brain is actually a seething bundle of ideas, and the only thing stopping them emerging into the daylight is you.

You will be sabotaging new ideas all the time:

- you might use up all your attention on things that inhibit the formation of new ideas

- you might shut ideas down before they're even born

- you might let ideas pop out, but then slam them back without giving them time to breathe

- you might not even dare to think of a new idea for fear of What People Will Say

This chapter, and the next three, are full of very simple techniques you can use to bypass this habit of sabotage and self criticism that we all have. You will be giving your creative self permission to flourish - in small ways at first, but once your brain gets in the habit of being creative, you will notice the process becomes easier.

How to be creative

I spent 2 years doing a Masters degree in online education, and my dissertation was on whether you can teach (and therefore learn) creativity. And the answer is yes, it can be taught. Actually, it's less a question of teaching creativity itself, more a question of removing the mental blocks we put up that inhibit the creativity that is there all the time.

I can show you many techniques in the next 4 chapters that will help you unlock your creativity, but I need a couple of things from you first.

1. *You need to be willing to make mistakes.* I know you hear this a lot, but I mean it. You have to be ready to press the shutter and really not care what the photo is like. Take a moment to think about that.

You don't have to share it, but you have to look at it without criticising yourself. You may criticise the photo, but you may NOT criticise the photographer.

2. *You need to stop calling your mistakes, "mistakes".* That implies they are wrong. How can that be, when you are on a journey, and they are essential steps along the way? The quickest way to take a photo you are proud of is actually to take 100 that you are not proud of - not to read 3 books, a monthly magazine and all my emails about how to take the photo you want to be proud of. So the photos you are not proud of are just that, nothing more. In fact you *can* be proud of them, because they are freeing your mind and getting you where you want to be.

You may criticise the photo, but you may NOT criticise the photographer

---

Setting limits to release creativity

Starting a piece of writing with a blank piece of paper, food shopping with no meal plan, garden design with no brief: all recipes for a long, tortuous, wasteful process to a single final (probably disappointing) outcome.

It's the same when you're about to take a photograph.

If you have a day set aside, but no goal, no definite idea of what you want to achieve, then more likely than not you'll try a bit of this, a bit of that, and finish up generally dissatisfied with everything.

But if you impose some artificial limits, your brain will respond like magic. Give the writer a list of objects they need to include, or a story arc, or an opening sentence, and they'll be off. Tell me I need 3 meals to be slow cooked, 2 packed lunches and a roast, and I'll have done the shopping in 20 minutes.

And let the garden designer know you have acid soil, you need a cutting garden and a wild flower area, and they've got somewhere to start.

As for the writer, the chef, the gardener, so for you. The first and simplest way to let your creative brain emerge is to set hard limits for it to work within.

In the homework for this chapter you'll find 12 different artificial constraints. You can try one or all of them. No cheating. You will run out of ideas at some point but you must keep going, keep taking photos, even though they are not going to be your best work. *The process of finding images will train the neurons in your brain that this is what you want it to do when you next start looking for images, and so then next time it will be easier.* (I have a psychology degree. This is true, I'm not making it up.)

Homework

Time restrictions

1. You must take a photograph every 5 minutes for an hour. Set an alarm, and you can spend no longer than 3 seconds looking for the image.

2. Go on a walk and take a photograph every 15 steps.

3. Do #1Day12Pics; take a photo every hour throughout the day.

4. You have 10 minutes to take 20 completely different photographs.

Place/subject restrictions

1. Throw something over your shoulder (this is just a marker, not your subject). Go and stand where it lands and take 20 different photographs from that spot.

2. Pick one thing (a chair, a toy, a vegetable, not a person) and take 20 completely different portraits of it.

3. Take photographs all day only from a toddler or dog's viewpoint.

4. Using only a piece of plain white paper as your subject, take 20 completely different photographs. (You can use a fresh piece of paper for each shot.)

Kit restrictions

1. 50 with 50: take 50 photos with your 50mm.

2. Create 20 completely different images using the same camera and lens, but on your smallest aperture.

3. What's the piece of kit you use least? Take it out and create 20 photos with it.

4. Take 20 different photos using a shutter speed of 1 second.

What about the camera controls?

I know you still might struggle with camera controls, and there are no short cuts. It's up to you how you want to do this section of the course. If you are constantly trying to remember apertures, or change shutter speeds, it will inhibit your creative brain. But you are also on a journey to learn to use your camera, so you might not want to forget everything you've learnt so far.

By all means, use your phone for these exercises, or stick your camera on Program, and have some fun. You can't be creative if you are worried.

But if you're up for it, you can take 5 or 10 minutes before the exercise to practise one (only one) manual control, and then use that one as you work through the exercise. For example, if you want to incorporate shallow depth of field, do some test shots with your camera on a large aperture first. Make sure you have enough light, and that all the other controls are working OK. Then leave your camera on that setting and forget it. Don't be tempted to change it during the exercise.

Stick a homework photo here (there are a lot of photos to take in this chapter so pick a favourite):

Checklist for Chapter 15

☐ I understand that technical skill goes hand in hand with creativity to create photographs that aren't just snapshots, and I must develop both in tandem

☐ I recognise that I have a unique set of creative ideas in my brain, just waiting for an opportunity to manifest themselves in my photographs

☐ I know that I must silence my inner critic and be willing to take some less creative photos on my journey (but I don't have to share these photos)

☐ I know that staring at a blank sheet of paper never helped anyone, and that artificial constraints can jump start the creative process

☐ I've done at least one of the homework projects

In my own words...

How was the process of finding photographs to take, and did it change throughout the exercises?

_____

_____

_____

_____

_____

_____

VISION IS THE ART OF SEEING THINGS INVISIBLE

~ JONATHAN SWIFT

16: Selective attention

Seeing as well as looking

If you've ever tried meditation, you'll be ahead of the game in this chapter. Directing your attention, bringing your wandering mind back to a focal point, and actually seeing the detail of what you're looking at is a skill every photographer needs to cultivate.

In this chapter

When you can't come up with any new ideas for your photography, or your images aren't as good as you expected, it might well be that you are just not directing your attention in the right way. Your brain might be busy with other priorities and thoughts, getting in the way of letting your eyes find new images, or spot distractions in the frame.

The good news is that you can train your brain to focus your attention where you want it - on the scene in front of you. It takes a bit of effort at first, but just like in the last chapter, the more you do it, the more your neural pathways will adapt to the new things you want them to do, and the more natural it will become.

This chapter is all about deliberately focussing your attention on the photograph you are about to take - not letting yourself be distracted by thinking about anything else. Not your to do list, or the weather, or how good or bad a photographer you think you are, just, "What photograph do I want to take, why, and how am I going to achieve it?".

Selective attention

Not focussing your attention is a problem at two distinct points in the birth of any photograph.

First, if you are mentally distracted when you are looking for photographs, you won't see all the creative opportunities in front of you.

Secondly, as you frame your image you might take shortcuts and believe your brain's interpretation over the reality. This happens when you make mistakes in exposure, or colour temperature. It also happens when you give the subject all your attention at the expense of the rest of the frame. Do you always take the time to check whether there is a lamppost sticking out of someone's head? Have you included far too much foreground? Is there a splash of red in the background that will distract from the subject?

Count the basketball throws

Have you done the 'count the basketball throws' selective attention test before? If not, navigate to this link and watch the video before you go on: https://www.youtube.com/watch?v=vJG698U2Mvo

Warm up exercise

Before you do the homework, have a go at this selective attention exercise:

First, look at something like a fork (tabletop size) for 5 whole minutes. Set a timer so your brain isn't distracted by worrying about the time. Sit and just look at it. See what happens to your thoughts, but don't worry when they wander. Just keep bringing your attention back to the object.

5 minutes is a long time to look at a fork, or whatever you chose. What happened? There's no right or wrong way to do this, nothing you should or shouldn't be thinking about - it's designed to help you become more aware of how easy it is to become distracted.

Homework

You don't need to do all the projects before you move on, but try at least one. The first set will help you to focus your attention on finding photographic opportunities. The second set will help you focus your attention on each frame you take.

Part 1 - finding photo opportunities

1. Leave your camera at home

Leave all your image making kit at home, and go for a walk. Look for photos on the way out and the way back. You will not be able to snap and move on - you are free to give each moment and opportunity your full attention.

Now do the walk again (exactly the same route), and take the photos. This works much better if you don't have your camera (or phone) with you at all the first time round. If you can, do leave everything at home rather than just having it with you but switched off.

2. Just start

Use your phone, or put your camera on auto, and just start taking photos. Focus on one small area in front of you. Don't worry about settings or exposure, light or composition. Take any photograph. Now move a bit and take another, until you have 20 shots.

Now you can either delete them all, or go through them and see what you've got. You should find that the act of starting to take photos will spark new ideas.

Part 2 - focus on the frame

3. 24 shots

Recreate the days of film: limit yourself to only 24 shots. And cover up your LCD completely so you don't sneak a peak as you go along. Wait until you get home to look at your photos. Or even better - leave it a couple of days like we used to have to.

When we only had 24 (or 36) shots, we made the most of every single one. Give it a go, whether you remember shooting film or not. You'll find you slow right down, and you'll start to pay attention to every single thing in the frame before you press the shutter.

4. Recreate someone else's image

Pick a famous photo, or just something that's caught your eye. Try and recreate it as closely as possible.

Look at light, camera position, and the relationship between elements.

5. Frame with your hands

One of the biggest problems of selective attention to overcome is not noticing things in the frame. Classic 'telegraph poles coming out of heads' shots happen because the photographer's attention was focussed on the person, not on the background. And because your eyes are approximately equivalent to a 50mm lens field of view, if you are not using a 50mm lens, you have to learn to direct your attention to what will actually be included in the frame - it might be more

than you can see naturally (if you're using a wide angle), or it might be less (telephoto).

For this exercise, make a frame with your hands, and try to compose your image within your artificial frame before you pick up the camera. Make yourself look all around the frame to check for distractions, and decide whether there's anything outside the frame that should be in it.

Stick a homework photo here (there are a lot of photos to take in this chapter so pick a favourite):

In my own words...

What happened when I watched a fork for 5 minutes?

_____

_____

_____

_____

_____

_____

Checklist for Chapter 16

☐ I understand that focussing my attention takes practice

☐ I know that I need to train myself not just to *look* at a scene but to *see* all the details that will be needed to find and take a photograph

☐ I've watched the counting the basketball throws video

☐ I've watched a fork for 5 minutes

☐ I've done at least one of the homework projects

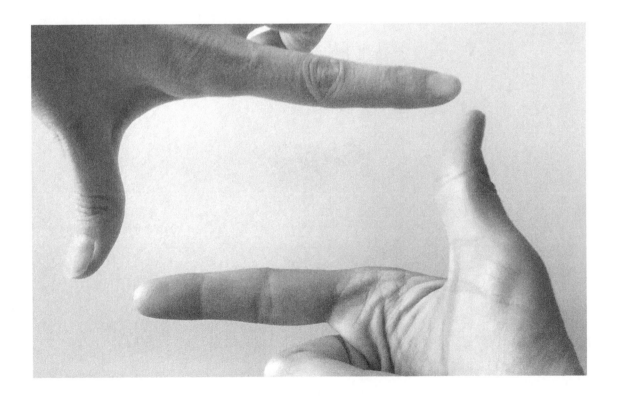

THE ARTIST WHO AIMS AT PERFECTION IN EVERYTHING ACHIEVES IT IN NOTHING

~ EUGENE DELACROIX

17: Nothing is original

You are original, not your photograph

"You don't make a photograph just with a camera. You bring to the act of photography all the pictures you have seen, the books you have read, the music you have heard, the people you have loved." *Ansel Adams*

In this chapter

One of the biggest stumbling blocks to overcome as a photographer is the feeling that it's all been done before, that you'll never create something new and original: What's the point?

Well, the point is that nothing is new; everything has been done before. All the photos have been taken. The landscapes, the viewpoints, the close ups, the portraits. Everything.

The only exception is when they invent something new. Drones gave us a new viewpoint, which was original for 5 minutes. The Big Stopper opened the door to all those seascapes where the sea is blurred into oblivion. Colour film was an advance on black and white.

So, new technology aside, you only have one idea to embrace in this chapter: you're probably not going to have a completely original idea for a photograph, so stop trying.

Instead, use your energy to make *unique* photographs. The idea you have might not be original, but the way you take the image will be unique to you, because no one else brings to the moment everything you have done, seen, read and experienced.

What makes you unique?

If everyone who reads this book took the same photo, I can guarantee they would all be different. Even if the brief was to take a photo of a piece of plain white paper, everyone would interpret it differently.

The idea in this chapter isn't a difficult one, but it does need saying, especially to people struggling to find their creative voice. All you need to do is let go of the need to be entirely original, and instead embrace the unique qualities that you - and no one else - can bring to a particular photograph.

Let me give you an example. I am a commercial and fine art botanical photographer, but for a long time I chose not to specialise in just flowers and gardens because I thought it would be too limiting. There could only be so many ways to photograph a flower, and they had surely all been done before?

So I kept my portrait business going alongside my flower clients, but discovered that my floral images weren't repetitive, and that I was constantly finding new ideas. Not necessarily entirely original ideas, but unique to me. I eventually closed my portrait business and haven't looked back since.

This might all sound like a nice idea, but conceptually quite vague, so here are three definite steps you can take to bring more of yourself to the photographs you take:

1. Remind yourself why you are different to everyone else.

2. Think about what subjects or style you are drawn to, and take more of that subject or in that style. Don't run away from subjects you like because you think they are easy - embrace your preferences.

3. Grow your experience, in a deliberate way. Travel if you can, read, look at paintings, listen to music. Try and stretch your comfort zone a bit - experience things you might not previously have chosen.

In my own words...

What makes me unique?

My favourite books:

_____

_____

Places I have visited:

_____

_____

Music I like to listen to:

_____

_____

Some things I have done that my next door neighbour hasn't:

_____

_____

Homework

How would your best friend, or someone close to you, describe you? Ask them to give you 3 words that come to mind when they think of you.

Now go out for the day to take photographs, and instead of trying to find new ideas or original photographs, aim to bring something of yourself to your images. What will you do that someone else might not? How can you show one of those 3 words in your final images? Take at least one image where you can say, "Yes, there's definitely something of me in that one."

You have permission to be unoriginal.

From this day on, don't let the fact that someone else has already taken the photograph you want to, stop you.

We often shy away from the obvious photograph, or the one we first think of, because it seems too easy. We think we should be trying harder or being more creative. But once in a while it's OK to do the easy thing, take the obvious shot. Because actually, what's obvious to you might not be obvious to the person standing next to you.

Being authentic, or unique, instead of striving for originality will help you uncover your own photographic style. It won't happen overnight. All you can do is promise yourself that you'll bring something of you to every photo you take. Your mood, your preferences, your history, your undivided attention. Next time you hear yourself complaining there's no point, and it's all been done before, tell yourself: "Yes, but not by me."

Some ideas

If this homework still seems a bit abstract, have a think about how your personality might affect the following decisions you make:

1. Viewpoint

There are an infinite number of viewpoints surrounding a subject, each giving a different feel to the final image. You might prefer a dramatic or unusual viewpoint, or maybe a safe, static one. There's no right answer - this is where you stamp your personality on your image.

2. Composition

Do you prefer things neatly ordered, or chaotic? Will you line things up carefully, or (equally carefully) make sure you've got a random effect? Perfectly symmetric or deliberately asymmetric? Frame full to bursting or minimalist?

3. Aperture

Do you find yourself always shooting wide open, or with front to back depth of field? Don't fight your preferences - use them deliberately. This homework is not one where you stretch yourself, it's one where you enjoy what you prefer.

4. Lens choice

Everyone has a go-to lens that they prefer. Maybe it's your 50mm or a telephoto. You might love the wide end of your range. Have a think about what that lens does that makes you reach for it first.

Stick a homework photo here (there are a lot of photos to take in this chapter so pick a favourite):

In my own words...

3 words that describe me, and how I can incorporate those into my photography:

_____

_____

_____

_____

_____

_____

Checklist for Chapter 17

☐ I understand that it's unlikely I'll take a truly original photograph - the first of its kind - unless I'm the first to use new technology

☐ I know that it doesn't matter

☐ I know I can bring my own personality and preferences to my photography to create images that are unique to me

☐ I know that even if the photograph I want to take has been taken a hundred times before, I should still take it and enjoy the fact I am drawn to a particular style or subject

☐ I've asked at least one person to describe me in 3 words

☐ I've had a go at taking a photograph that is unique to me, even if I found this homework a bit vague or abstract

---

Remember:

1. Don't be afraid of taking photos that seem too easy.

2. Embrace the subjects you love and enjoy taking photos of them.

3. Your preferences form the foundations of developing your own photographic style.

4. Put to one side the thankless task of searching for originality of ideas, and instead concentrate on authenticity and uniqueness.

IF YOU HEAR A VOICE
WITHIN YOU SAY 'YOU
CANNOT PAINT,' THEN BY
ALL MEANS PAINT, AND
THAT VOICE WILL BE
SILENCED

~ VINCENT VAN GOGH

18: Finding inspiration

Sometimes you do need a new idea

In the last chapter you reinforced the fact you should embrace your own preferences, and make photographs that are unique just because you took them. Sometimes though, you want to try something new to you, and this chapter will help you find new ideas.

In this chapter

Half way through my Masters degree I had to come up with a completely original research proposal. It could be on anything at all to do with education. I was like a rabbit in the headlights – I froze, and for 2 weeks could not come up with a single idea.

A year later, research completed, I discovered that in giving me free reign to do what I wanted, my tutors were not doing me any favours at all. They would have done better to give me some kind of boundary.

I ended up researching whether creativity could be taught, and apart from discovering that yes, it can, I also pieced together 3 principles that come up again and again in the area of creative breakthroughs.

In this chapter I'll share the 3 principles with you, and show you how you can apply them to your own photography. Next time you need a new idea, do these 3 steps and I guarantee a breakthrough will happen.

The 3 step process

Set limits

Before you start, if there are none, make some limits up. Your brain is a million times* more productive when it has boundaries than when it is free to wander where it wants. For example:

Time: set a time limit, preferably around the 20 minute mark, by which time you will stop searching for new ideas.

Prompts: pick a random word and use it to trigger ideas.

Quota: you have to come up with a set number of new ideas.

made up statistic

The 3 steps

1. The first is 20 minutes of pure brainstorming, working to the limits you have set. Turn off your internal critic – no idea is wrong and absolutely no criticism is allowed, because criticism inhibits your creative flow.

2. Next, spend 20 minutes with your practical hat on. Now you can go through your ideas, edit them, and discard any that are really, genuinely impractical. Don't be too hasty though: the most creative ideas seemed crazy at one point.

3. Last, if you need it, you use an incubation stage to refine your ideas, or generate more if you need them. Honestly, this works. First, articulate your question; eg "I need 3 photo project ideas." Then let the question incubate while you go for a walk or a drive. Or take a shower. If you leave your brain simmering the problem whilst you do something very mundane that doesn't need you to think about anything else, its neurons will do their work, trigger new connections and spit out a creative breakthrough.

Do not multitask

Multitasking doesn't work: it's inefficient and you shouldn't do it. Turn off all distractions, do not think about anything else and concentrate only on the task in hand. It's only 20 minutes of your life.

Homework: come up with a new photo idea

Brainstorming stage

1. Spend 20 minutes brainstorming. Don't forget, there are no wrong answers. And don't let your practical brain have an opinion at this stage - no saying to yourself, "I can't take a photo of the Eiffel Tower even though I've always wanted to, because I'm not in Paris." The question at this stage is, what photograph do you *want* to take, not what *can* you take.

Even if you already know exactly what new photograph you want to take today, do the exercise anyway. You'll come up with plenty of new ideas.

Write down all your ideas. You might find some ideas trigger others, or long lost photo projects are remembered. You might remember you once wanted to do something with your old family photos, or you saw a project you wanted to try in a magazine.

Don't forget - absolutely no editing at this stage. Anything goes.

Editing stage

2. Now you can edit. Cross things off that are physically impossible (but not without thinking about potential workarounds first - maybe you could recreate Paris in your kitchen). Delete things you don't fancy so much, and then make a list of what's left in a vague order of what you'd most like to do. Then pick the first one and do it.

Incubation stage

3. If you struggled to come up with ideas, now is the time for a walk, a shower or a drive. Say the question out loud; "What new photograph do I want to take today?", then off you go. Don't force yourself to think about it or worry about not having any ideas. Put it to the back of your mind and get on with the mundane activity. (Must be done alone - having company is a distraction.)

Stick the photo you took here:

In my own words...

What happened when I tried the 3 step process?

_____

_____

_____

_____

_____

_____

Checklist for Chapter 18

☐ I understand that when I'm stuck for ideas, there is a 3-step process I can use to generate new ideas

☐ I know that when I'm in the brainstorming step, I must not edit my ideas - anything goes

☐ I know that I can only edit my ideas in step 2

☐ I know that my brain will incubate ideas if I let it, by going for a walk or a drive, or doing a mundane activity

☐ I know that I must not have distractions while I'm doing this exercise

☐ I've done the 3 step process and taken a photo that I thought up as a result of the exercise

End of Part 4 - test yourself

Consolidate your knowledge by taking these photos. Take as long as you like to work through the list.

☐ take a shot at the same time every day for a month

☐ photograph the same thing in the same place every hour for a day - you can only change your viewpoint

☐ go for a walk and take 10 eye catching photos using only your phone

☐ look up now, and then take a compelling photo using only something within your field of view

☐ shoot the same subject from a bird's eye view and a snail's eye view

☐ make a fascinating photo that is shot from your head height

☐ compose an image and choose your settings as normal, but shoot with your eyes closed

☐ focus your attention on just the background for a whole day

☐ take 10 photos where you took 10 deep breaths before you pressed the shutter

☐ indulge yourself for a week - only take photos of things you love, on settings you are comfortable with, in a style that comes easily

☐ next time you are driving, walking or showering, think about what you'd like to photograph next

End of Part 4 project

PROJECT: Make something meaningful

Start with a person, a poem, a place or a painting that means something to you. Create a photograph that captures an element of what it means to you, however small.

Use the creativity exercises from Part 4 to percolate a few ideas. Let them rest, and come back to them. Then use the process from the end of the Part 3 project to plan your settings, composition and lighting.

Print your photograph and put it up on the wall.

What next?

1. Well done. Congratulations for getting this far. Take a moment and think about what you know now that you didn't know when you started.

2. You can now call yourself a photographer. If you want to carry on making progress for the rest of the year, have a look at Book 2. Details at AYearWithMyCamera.com/Book2.

3. Help me improve the next edition of this book. There's a short, anonymous feedback form here, please fill it in (especially if you didn't understand something, or found a typo): http://bit.ly/AYWMCfeedback

4. Keep practising. Go back and try some of the exercises again. Do you need to revisit the histograms, or the exposure triangle chapter? Did you finish all of the end-of-Part projects? Share your images (#AYearWithMyCamera).

END OF BOOK 1: TEST YOURSELF

1.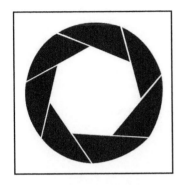

This aperture is most likely to be:

A f2.8

B f22

C f32

2.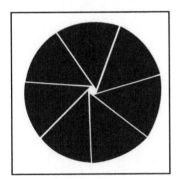

This aperture is most likely to be:

A f5.6

B f8

C f22

3.

Which of these size apertures best represents f16?

A    B   C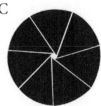

4. Which of these apertures gives the largest depth of field?

A f8   B f16   C f11

5. Which of these apertures gives the smallest depth of field?

A f22   B f11   C f16

6. Which of these is the fastest shutter speed?

A 1/4 sec   B 1/2 sec   C 1 sec

7. Which of these is the slowest shutter speed?

A 1/1000   B 1/2000   C 1/4000

8. To go one full stop faster (less light) from a shutter speed of 1/60, what do you need?

A 1/80   B 1/100   C 1/125

9. To go one full stop slower (more light) from a shutter speed of 1/320, what do you need?

A 1/125   B 1/160   C 1/250

10. To change settings but keep the same exposure from f8, 1/125 and ISO 200, which settings can you use?

A f11, 1/60, ISO 100   B f16, 1/60, ISO 400   C f4, 1/60, ISO 100

11. To go 2 stops more light than f5.6, 1/250 and ISO 200, which combination can you use?

A f4, 1/60, ISO 100   B f11, 1/1000, ISO 50   C f11, 1/125, ISO 200

12. Which of these is the symbol for spot metering?

A    B    C

13. Which histogram best represents a chequerboard (64 squares - half black, half white)?

A    B    C

14. Match the image to the histogram

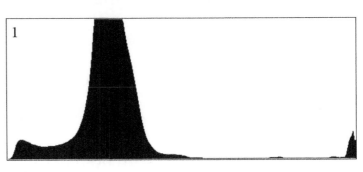

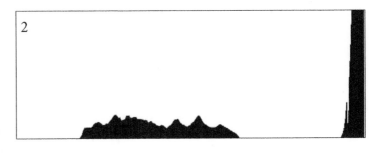

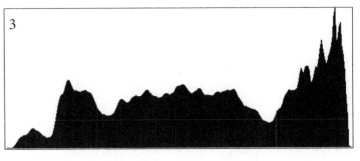

15. Can you take these photographs?

- [ ] an image where you blur the background

- [ ] an image where you freeze a moving subject

- [ ] an image where you blur a moving subject

- [ ] an image with both the subject and background in focus

- [ ] an image shot inside with no flash, and not underexposed

- [ ] a white subject on a white background

- [ ] a truly eyecatching image

- [ ] a dynamic image

- [ ] a static image

- [ ] an aesthetically pleasing image

- [ ] a back lit image with the subject correctly exposed

- [ ] a side lit image to bring out texture

- [ ] an image taken indoors with no orange colour cast

- [ ] an image with a high dynamic range where you chose to expose for the highlights

- [ ] a sunset that isn't too dark or too blue

- [ ] an image that reflects you or your style

- [ ] a photograph you are proud of

APPENDIX 1a: Apertures - full, half and third stops

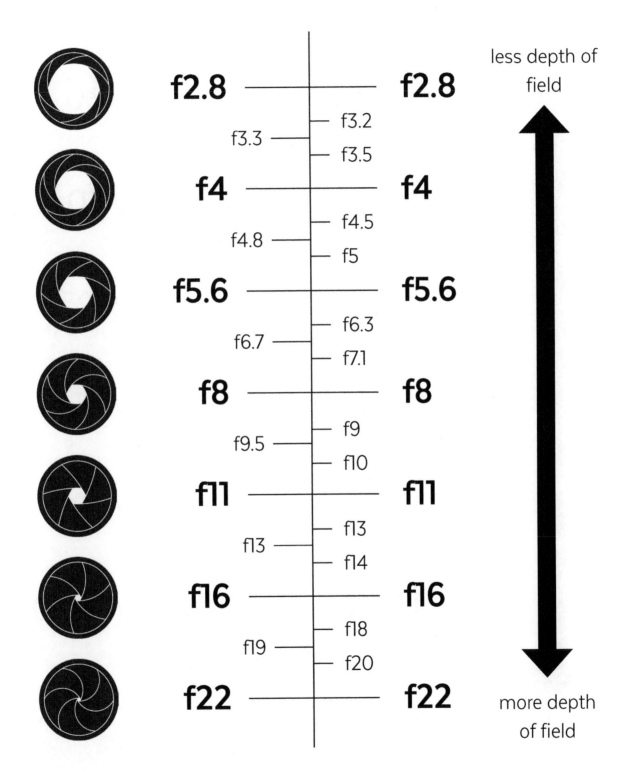

f2.8

f3.3
f3.2
f3.5

f4

f4.8
f4.5
f5

f5.6

f6.7
f6.3
f7.1

f8

f9.5
f9
f10

f11

f13
f13
f14

f16

f19
f18
f20

f22

f2.8

f4

f5.6

f8

f11

f16

f22

less depth of field

more depth of field

163

APPENDIX 1b: Shutter speed (fractions of a second) - full, half and third stops

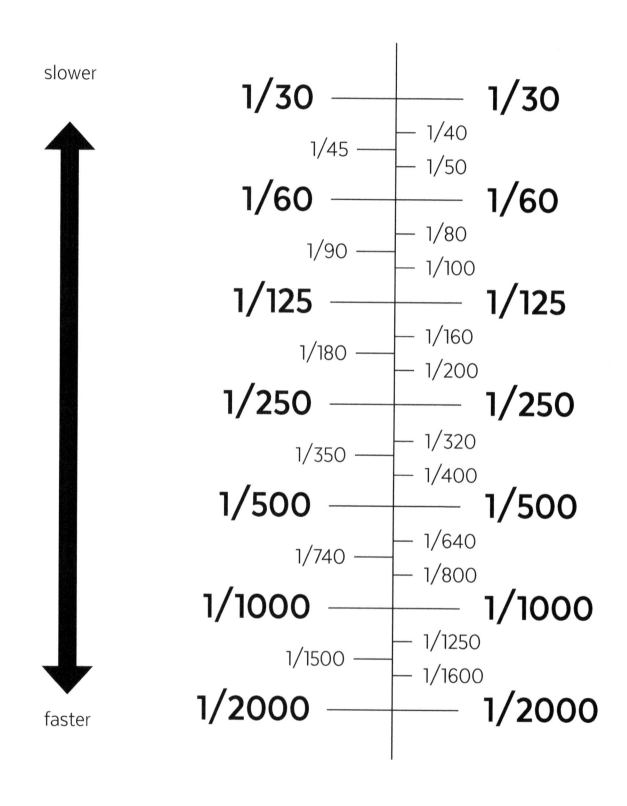

APPENDIX 1c: ISO - full, half and third stops

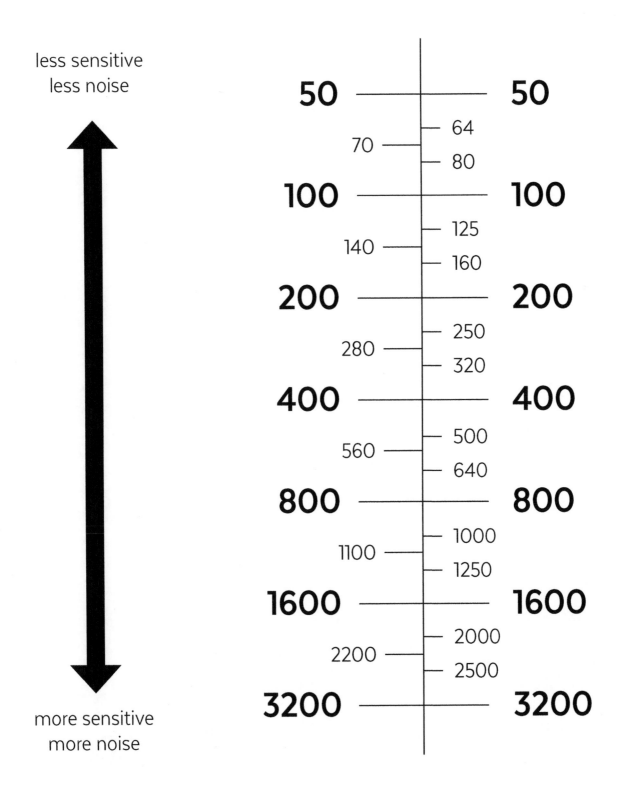

less sensitive
less noise

more sensitive
more noise

50		50
	64	
70	80	
100		100
	125	
140	160	
200		200
	250	
280	320	
400		400
	500	
560	640	
800		800
	1000	
1100	1250	
1600		1600
	2000	
2200	2500	
3200		3200

APPENDIX 2: RAW, JPEGs and resolution

RAW and JPEG

The quick takeaway is this: *make sure you are shooting either "large JPEGs" or RAW*. Look up in your manual how to change this, and check before you start. If in doubt, choose large JPEG.

The reason is image quality. If you are shooting smaller JPEGs, your file sizes will be smaller, but your image quality will be correspondingly smaller. You won't be able to print your photographs so big, and you won't be able to make many edits before the images start to deteriorate noticeably.

RAW files are just that - all the raw information that the camera collects, with no edits or changes made. JPEG files are smaller than RAW files. With JPEGs, the camera makes a few edits (contrast, brightness, sharpness, colour), compresses the file and then throws away all the information it doesn't need any more. JPEG files look better straight out of the camera, but RAW files keep a lot more detail so that you can edit them later.

If you are never, ever going to edit your files, shoot large JPEG.

If you shoot a lot of continuous shutter images (where you press the shutter and it fires off 7 or 8 images a second), shoot large JPEG.

If you don't have much storage, or time to upload and download your files, shoot large JPEG.

If you ever want to edit your files, and storage isn't an issue, shoot RAW.

Resolution

Digital photographs are made up of pixels. A pixel is a tiny square of colour, so small that you can't see individual pixels just with your eye.

The resolution of an image is simply the number of pixels it has. If the image is 1,000 pixels along the top edge and 500 pixels tall, the total number of pixels is 1,000 x 500, which is 500,000. That's the same as 0.5 MP (megapixels).

Your camera probably takes images that are at least 8 MP in size (if you are shooting Large JPEGs). That's 3,264 x 2,448 pixels.

Resolution is important when it comes to printing. If you want to print a 6x4 inch photograph, you'll need at least 1800 x 1200 pixels (2.1 MB). If you have been shooting Small JPEG or thumbnail size, you might not have a big enough file to print. This is because printers use about 300 pixels for every inch printed (called "ppi" or "dpi" - pixels per inch, or dots per inch). So to print at 6 inches long, you need 6 inches x 300 pixels = 1800 pixels. And 4 inches x 300 pixels = 1200. 1600 x 1200 = 2.1MB.

APPENDIX 3: Lenses

What is focal length?

The number on your lens followed by "mm" is the focal length; 35mm, 50mm, 200mm. Technically, this measurement is the the distance between the lens and the sensor, when the subject is in focus.

Focal length affects the angle of view, or how much of the scene you can capture in your photograph. A wide-angle lens has a smaller focal length, like 28mm or 35mm, and lets you include a lot of the scene in the final image. In fact, wide angle lenses give you a field of view wider than the human eye - the camera can see, side to side, more than the eye.

The lens which is closest to the human angle of view is the 50mm lens, and it is sometimes referred to as a "standard prime". Longer lenses, like 200mm or 400mm, are called telephoto lenses. They bring distant subjects closer, but have a narrower angle of view.

Primes vs zooms

Prime lenses have just one measurement - 50mm, 100mm. Zoom lenses have a range - 18-55mm or 70-210mm. With a prime lens, the angle of view is fixed. The benefit of a zoom lens is that you can change angles of view just by twisting the barrel. An 18-55mm zoom will be a wide-angle at one end, and a normal angle of view at the other.

So why doesn't everyone just buy zooms? The main reason is the cost of having large maximum apertures in zoom lenses. You'll be aware by now that having the option to use a very wide aperture (f2.8, f1.8) is important to photographers. It's very expensive to manufacture lenses with wider apertures, and even more expensive if the lens is a zoom. So typically, zoom lenses have an inferior maximum aperture. Cheaper zoom lenses won't even have a fixed maximum aperture for the whole zoom - it will reduce as you zoom. For example the maximum aperture at the wide end of an 18-55mm zoom might be f3.5, but at 55mm it might go down to f5.6. A 50mm f1.8 lens costs about two and half times less than an 18-55mm f3.5-f5.6 lens and, for a photographer wanting to use wide apertures, is infinitely more useful.

The other advantage of using prime lenses is weight. Zoom lenses might be convenient because you don't have to keep changing lenses, but they are big and heavy.

Third party lenses and second hand lenses

If you can't afford a wide maximum aperture lens from your camera manufacturer, consider third party lenses and second hand lenses. I recommend doing some online research for third party lenses before you buy, to see what's been said by others. And with second hand lenses the biggest risks are that it has been dropped or scratched.

Full frame vs cropped frame

In the days of 35mm film cameras, the size of the negative was 24mm x 36mm. It was called 35mm because the total width of the film, including the perforations, was 35mm. Nowadays, if a camera's sensor is approximately 24mm x 36mm, it's referred to as "full frame". If it is smaller, it is referred to as "cropped frame", or having a "crop factor". If you don't know whether your camera is full frame or cropped, it's probably cropped. Full frame cameras are more expensive.

If your sensor is full frame, then your lenses will work as advertised. A 50mm lens will give a 50mm field of view. If your sensor is cropped, then you have to apply the crop factor to find out exactly how your lens will behave. To all intents and purposes it's easier just to look through the viewfinder and see what happens - that's what your field of view is. But if you are buying a new lens, it's worth doing a bit of maths and working out how your new lens might behave.

First, look up online what the crop factor of your camera is (just Google it - eg, "What's the crop factor of an XT1?").

The XT1 has a crop factor of around 1.5. This means I need to multiply the focal length of my lenses by 1.5 to see how they will behave. A 50mm x 1.5 becomes a 75mm. A nice wide 18mm becomes a less wide 27mm. And a medium telephoto 200mm becomes a long telephoto 300mm.

Macro lenses

A macro lens is probably the first specialist lens most people buy. They have smaller closest focussing distances than their non-macro counterparts. They are usually prime lenses, and can be used as normal primes as well as for close up photography.

DO THIS NOW:

Join A Year With My Camera via email, and get a reminder email every Thursday. It'll help you stay on track, remind you to pick up your camera and let you know about any new projects and meetups.

Join at AYearWithMyCamera.com

The two pages that follow can be used for the homework in the first chapter:

Printed in Great Britain
by Amazon

35096525R00113